To my mother, Elizabeth Lemos, who always made the kitchen the heart of our home

Acknowledgments

WISE PERSON ONCE NOTED that it takes a village to raise a child. A book is no different. The village of people who helped to bring this book to completion are numerous, including most notably the homeowners who let us into their homes and shared their kitchens and lives with us.

I thank the many people at The Taunton Press who helped to shape this book, beginning with Maria Taylor, Maureen Graney, and Paula Schlosser, who brought me into this project in its earliest phases and contributed greatly to the concept. But this book would never have gotten done without the hard work of my editors, Erica Sanders-Foege and Pam Thomas, who brought it all the way to completion. And many thanks to Robyn Doyon-Aitken, who stayed on top of the many details that went into putting it together.

I'd also like to thank Ken Gutmaker for his outstanding photography, as well as the many architects, designers, and contractors who were extremely generous with their time and knowledge and without whom these beautiful kitchens would probably not have come to be.

Finally, thanks to my wife, Rachel, and my children, Elizabeth and Simon, who put up with the consuming passion this book became for a few months.

Contents

PETER LEMOS

Kitchens
for the Rest of Us

From the Kitchen You Have to the Kitchen You Love

Photographs *by* Ken Gutmaker

The Taunton Press

The Taunton Press, Inc., 63 South Main Street, PO Box 5506, Newtown, CT 06470-5506
e-mail: tp@taunton.com

Kitchens for the Rest of Us was previously published in hardcover in 2005 by The Taunton Press, Inc.

Editor: Erica Sanders-Foege
Jacket/Cover design: Alexander Isley, Inc.
Interior design: Lori Wendin
Layout: Lori Wendin
Illustrator: Chuck Lockhart
Photographer: Ken Gutmaker

Library of Congress Cataloging-in-Publication Data
Lemos, Peter.
  Kitchens for the rest of us : from the kitchen you have to the kitchen you love / Peter Lemos ;
photographs by Ken Gutmaker.
    p. cm.
  ISBN-10: 1-56158-759-1 (hardcover)
  ISBN-13: 978-1-56158-759-9 (hardcover)
  ISBN-10: 1-56158-951-9 (paperback)
  ISBN-13: 978-1-56158-951-7 (paperback)
  1. Kitchens--Remodeling. I. Title.
  TH4816.3.K58L46 2005
  747.7'97--dc22
                              2005008227
Printed in the United States of America
10 9 8 7 6 5 4 3 2 1

The following manufacturers/names appearing in *Kitchens for the Rest of Us* are trademarks: Alkco®, Amana®, American Standard®, Avonite®, Blanco®, Bosch®, Broan®, Brookhaven®, Bulthaup®, CaesarStone®, Cambria®, Chicago Faucets®, Concinnity®, Corian®, Country Floors®, Dacor®, DCS™, DuPont®, Dynasty®, Earthstone®, Elkay®, Faber®, Fisher & Paykel®, Flos®, Formica®, Franke®, Frigidaire®, General Electric®, Grohe®, Halo®, Heath®, Huggy Bear's Cupboards®, IMC®, Jade®, Jenn-Air®, John Boos™, Juno®, KitchenAid®, Kohler®, KWC®, Lightolier®, Marmoleum®, Maytag®, Miele®, Moen®, Nevamar®, Pionite®, Sigma®, Silestone®, Sub-Zero®, Swanstone®, Thermador®, Viking®, Walker & Zanger®, Wicanders®, Wilsonart®, Wilsonart Earthstone™, Wolf®, Wood-Mode®, Woodharbor®, Zodiaq®

From the Kitchen
You Have
to the Kitchen
You Love

The Hardest-Working Room in the House

●●●●● Here's how to get **THIS**

When you start with **THIS**

before The original Victorian kitchen featured many charming historic details that were unfortunately packed into a too-small space.

after Restored and reproduced Victorian woodwork and traditional soapstone counters are mixed with modern materials to achieve this classic, family-friendly kitchen.

HEN MY TWO KIDS COME HOME from school each day, the first thing they do is head to the kitchen. It is the first place I go when I wake up in the morning and the last place I turn off the lights before I go to bed. It is where our mail gets sorted, the phone messages stored, medicines dispensed, groceries processed in, and garbage and recycling processed out. The kitchen is the hardest-working single room in our home, as I am sure it is in yours.

If we are to believe many of the magazines we read, though, the key to a good kitchen is size—that our kitchens should spread ever outward. But most of us need something that functions well on a modest scale. We are looking for kitchens that live up to the demands of this hardworking reality, with enough room for us to cook and gather with relative ease, but not much more size than we require to create a balance of comfort and efficiency.

The Five Essential Steps

Think of a remodeling project as a series of small individual projects, or steps. This will help to focus your ideas and sort through the options.

1. TAKING STOCK

Look around your present kitchen and figure out what you most want to change and what you might like to keep. Plan how much money to spend, and prioritize the wish list.

2. FINDING YOUR STYLE

Imagine the look you want your new kitchen to have. Traditional or contemporary? Urban "ultra-modern" or country "casual"?

3. WORKING WITH PROS

Call in the pros—architects, contractors, kitchen designers. Do some research; get recommendations. Even if you don't hire them, make sure to at least consult with them.

4. DEFINING YOUR SPACE

Decide how you want your new space to be organized. Architects and contractors will help you create an efficient plan, which will ultimately save you money.

5. MAKING IT HAPPEN

Put all of these major decisions together and fill in the details—flooring, lighting, color, furniture, etc. Work out the finishing touches.

above Crisp, new stainless-steel appliances and classically elegant finishing details such as vintage green tiles produce an inspired mix of new and old in the compact space of this remodeled Houston kitchen.

How each of us chooses to shape that optimum space is the question at the heart of this book. What each of us wants in a new kitchen grows out of our own particular blend of fond memories, culinary ambitions, domestic dreams, practical needs, and magazine-driven fantasies. This book will help decipher this mix of emotions and aspirations, to sort out what's possible from what is not, to separate the practical from the frivolous, to filter through the seemingly infinite range of design and product choices available today, and to, quite simply, help you get your own kitchen project started.

The 20 newly remodeled and tightly designed kitchens in this book emphasize function, craft, and intelligent planning over size and extravagance. They have all been built within typical-sized spaces (about 150 sq. ft.) in real homes, on real budgets (most of the remodeled kitchens cost between $30,000 and $50,000). From these practical examples, there is much to be inspired by as you pursue your own mix of dreams, hopes, and needs. Consider the emergency-room nurse in California who designed her kitchen to replicate the efficiency of a hospital; or the professional cook in Wyoming who holds classes in his kitchen; or the Vermont family that created a Victorian kitchen in their hundred-year-old home.

How to go about designing and crafting your own new kitchen depends on the resources and space available to you. Begin by taking a close look at how much money you can and want to spend on a new kitchen. Remember that these are separate categories; you do not have to spend everything you can on a new kitchen to get what you want. As these kitchens demonstrate, creative planning and smart design deliver as much—if not more—function and pleasure as a fat budget. By making the most of the kitchen space available and by mixing uses in the spaces around the kitchen, it is possible to get much more bang from every remodeling buck.

above With spice racks on the door and several tightly packed roll-out shelves, this pantry cupboard maximizes the limited storage space of a small Berkeley, California, kitchen.

above Dedicated storage features like the dish rack, cubbies, and microwave niche in the cabinets of this California kitchen meet the precise needs of the homeowners and help to make the space uniquely theirs.

taking stock

above Shelving at varying heights and depths provides hidden storage in this pantry that was remodeled on a budget.

eVERY SUCCESSFUL KITCHEN REMODELING PROJECT begins with a good understanding of what works and what doesn't. Look at each specific part of your existing kitchen (cabinets, appliances, countertops, backsplashes, sinks, faucets, floors, paint colors, windows, lights, and furnishings), and then consider how all of the pieces work together. You may want to preserve or duplicate some things (a handy pantry, for example), or you may want to eliminate or change other things (such as an inconvenient doorway). This process helps you understand how much to change, and the actual importance of each change. Create a wish list, then prioritize it, figuring out which things you really must have and which things you can live without.

With this balance sheet of goals and desires in hand, outline a rough budget. The cost of a kitchen remodeling project can be anywhere from $50 to $400 per sq. ft., depending on what you want, where you live, and who you hire to help you. Or to put it more concretely, for a typical 10-ft. by 12-ft. kitchen, new cabinets could cost anywhere from a few thousand dollars for stock cabinets from a discount store to tens of thousands of dollars for custom cabinets made with expensive materials. Appliances cost from hundreds of dollars each to several thousand for the highest-end products. Add more floor area or throw in some major physical alterations or posh materials, and the cost will quickly climb. Figure how much—if at all—you want to expand, and research the relative costs of the appliances and cabinets you would like. Then do the math.

Two rules of thumb: You should not spend more than 10 percent of your home's value on a new kitchen, and, when you sell your home, expect to get back only 80 percent to 90 percent of what you invested.

above If it works, keep it. This remodeled Philadelphia kitchen uses the hanging pot rack from the old kitchen that the homeowner found to be a great organizing tool.

reality check

■ When drawing up a balance sheet of the assets and deficiencies of your existing kitchen, remember to include these general elements of kitchen design:

Size. Is the overall space enough to fit your needs and desires? Are specifics like the refrigerator, stove, and storage spaces as big as you'd like?

Function. Does your current kitchen allow for good flow, storage, work space, lighting, and windows? Can you find everything easily?

Looks. Do you like the way your kitchen looks? If so, how can you replicate that feeling? If not, what can you change to get the look you want?

Comfort. Do you feel at home in your kitchen? Can you cook with ease? Do you and others want to spend time there?

Features. What specific features do you want most? A pro-style range? Gas burners or electric? Wall ovens or a range? An island? A breakfast bar? A walk-in pantry?

left In order to afford the special cabinets for this baking center, the owners decided not to tear down and rebuild the curved wall it abuts.

finding your style

F YOU LIVE IN A VICTORIAN TOWNHOUSE or a Craftsman bungalow, determining what style your new kitchen will be may not pose such a big question. Then again, this is an issue that goes beyond cookie-cutter definitions of style. It's important to include lifestyle in the equation. So begin by researching style options in books and magazines but also in showrooms and kitchen centers. Consider options that fit your house as well as the way you live in your kitchen. Many other decisions will follow from this one: materials, finishes, colors, and to some extent budget. Most important, the professionals you hire should have experience working in the style you want.

The décor of a new kitchen will be determined mainly by the style of cabinets. They create the largest single visual component of a kitchen's design, so begin here. Then move on to considering countertops, backsplashes, appliances, flooring, and wall color. Create a scrapbook of ideas torn from magazines or copied from books. Another great idea is to keep a "Don't" scrapbook of things you don't like. This will help focus your thinking and make it easier to communicate these ideas to spouses, designers, and contractors. It is also a great way to screen professionals to find out if they like what you like.

Wherever possible, visit showrooms that contain full kitchens with appliances and accessories, instead of those with just cabinet

above Staggered cabinets and a surfboard-shaped peninsula table add to the breezy style of this California contemporary kitchen.

left Carefully conceived period details in the woodwork and hand-painted cabinetry are incorporated in the storage niche above the refrigerator in this modern Craftsman kitchen.

above This cozy corner table wrapped in warm wainscoting was the homeowner's way of making the strong style statement she wanted, while boosting the function of her new kitchen.

mock-ups. It's important to see how various aspects of a style interact. This will also help you visualize mixing and matching elements of different styles, an increasingly popular approach. Finally, visiting showrooms is a great reality check for the budget. Seeing real kitchens with price tags attached will help you evaluate what different styles, finishes, and types of construction cost relative to each other.

working with pros

above Paint colors are a cost-effective way to add pizzazz to a kitchen. An inexpensive consultation with a color designer yielded this multi-hued cabinet color scheme.

ONCE YOU HAVE A GENERAL IDEA of features, styles, and cost, start talking to architects, contractors, and designers. In fact, it's best to talk to several if you have time. Bear in mind that good kitchen professionals tend to be booked up months in advance. You want to be on their radar as soon as possible. It's a good idea, too, to pick their brains before you become too wed to one strategy or another. These conversations can also help provide a preliminary check on time and cost considerations.

Even if you are considering doing the remodeling work yourself, it's still a good idea to talk to some experts. You may discover that they can save you more time and money through their professional connections and discounts and their familiarity with the work than you can by doing it yourself. Some may even let you do certain parts of the job, such as demolition, sanding, tiling, or painting.

Start by getting recommendations from friends. Equally important, find out who they may have avoided and why. Be wary of kitchen-remodeling shops that hook you up with someone who is mainly a salesperson and who wants to talk immediately about estimates and contracts. Deal with somebody who starts with ideas and options. Be especially wary if they offer to arrange financing for you. In most cases, you will end up paying more than if you arrange financing yourself. In any case, it is simply better to keep these aspects of your renovation separate. This is important: *You want to control the money so you can control the job.*

above The couple who renovated this kitchen chose a design/build team whose specialty is the clever wicket, a storage door in a door.

pros to know

■ Here are the professionals you'll want to consider first. They will hire or refer specific tradespeople like plumbers, electricians, tilers, and finish carpenters.

Architect. By training, he or she is ready to deal with the structural and spatial aspects of remodeling and tends to be knowledgeable about what's new in design, materials, and technologies. Fees range from 5 percent to 15 percent of a project's total cost, depending on how much involvement the architect has.

Contractor. The contractor is the one who makes it all happen, and some even offer design services, which if they are good can save you money. Good contractors are in demand and can be booked up months in advance but are worth the wait. Fees are usually built in to the bid they give you, so getting competitive bids can keep costs down.

Kitchen Designer. A good alternative to an architect, though usually not qualified to handle structural matters. Look for designers certified by the National Kitchen and Bath Association (NKBA). Fees are about 5 percent to 10 percent of the cost of the project.

Cabinet Company. Many local specialty cabinet companies incorporate full kitchen design, installation, and contracting into their services. Some are also certified designers.

left By doing much of the extensive demolition and light finishing work themselves, the couple who owns this kitchen managed to stay on their tight budget.

defining your space

above Good design sometimes means making a virtue out of a necessity. In this case, the fact that the range needed to move out 4 in. to accommodate a vent pipe behind the wall became a design asset, creating better access to the back burners.

ERE, WE TACKLE THE SIZE, location, and layout of your new kitchen. If space limitations have been a problem in the present kitchen and they can't be resolved in the existing space with better-organized storage and layout, think about where to gain space. Do you want to move out existing exterior walls with a bump-out or a full addition? Do you want to expand into an adjoining space? Do you want to relocate your new kitchen to a different space within the house? Or can you accomplish your goals by reorganizing your kitchen and adjoining spaces into a combined new space?

How these questions are answered will have a significant bearing on the budget. More space always means more money. If you plan to move around interior bearing walls to gain space, you will add still more money to the budget, since walls need to be replaced with structural pillars and beams. If you want to move exterior walls, you will jack the costs up even higher, plus the outside of the house in the area of reconstruction will have to be refinished.

To get a handle on the spatial arrangement that makes the most sense, lay out the plan of your existing kitchen on paper, then redraw it the way you would like it to be even if you have already hired a designer or architect. Think about the orientation of the kitchen to the sun, to windows, and to other rooms. Consider how traffic flows in and out of the kitchen and into nearby spaces. How much of a connection do you want with other rooms or outdoor areas? As you do this, start to prioritize how the space should be allocated within the new kitchen.

left The homeowner measured every inch of her small kitchen, took a hard look at how much she really needed to store, and then designed this custom system of hanging shelves.

Cut out movable templates for major components such as cabinets, appliances, islands, and furniture to try out various alternatives. Be sure to include adequate floor area for movement in and around the kitchen in between all these elements. The general rule is that the passages between counters or between counters and islands should be 42 in. to 48 in. wide to allow for people and (sometimes hot) trays to pass each other safely and for refrigerator, oven, and dishwasher doors and drawers to open.

above This large pass-through opens up an attractive sight line to the string of hanging lamps and display shelves beyond.

left As a result of the remodel, this Victorian kitchen is closer and more connected to the dining room.

making it happen

above After adding a wall of windows and French doors to their kitchen, this couple created a space that opened up to the great outdoors.

ONCE THE LARGE ISSUES HAVE BEEN WORKED OUT—style, space, cost, and who is doing the work—direct your attention to the many details that will turn your new kitchen into a reality. From paint colors and cabinet hardware to lighting, furniture, and accessories, the little things that flesh out the design of your kitchen will make a huge difference in the finished product.

The most important detail to attend to, though, is the schedule of work. Even though most tasks may be handled by the pros, the more you know, the more you will be able to adjust and the more control you will have. Your contractor should be able to give you a preliminary schedule for such things as design processes, obtaining permits, and demolition.

Now be prepared to wait. Remodeling projects rarely start when they are supposed to and, even more, rarely finish when planned. Previously unknown plumbing, dangerously old wiring, newly discovered rot, out-of-plumb walls, and even the slow genesis of a few better ideas will all conspire to push back the completion dates. Brace yourself for this. Share the schedule with family members so they are not rudely surprised. If you feel frustrated and out of control when things go awry, think how your family will feel with even less information and input. Anticipating and passing on changes in the schedule will take a lot of the bumps out of the process for everyone.

left Small details in the design of this island, such as the dark stain, furniture-style legs, raised china cabinet, and carefully positioned trio of hanging lamps, make it the focal point of the kitchen.

above Stainless-steel wall panels and a wood-fired bread oven are two of the restaurant-style finishing touches that make this kitchen, which is owned by a chef, unique.

"Like cooking in a time capsule from 1934"

A Colonial revival for a 21st-century family

HOW DO YOU MAKE A HOUSE MORE FUNCTIONAL without diminishing its original appeal? That was the situation facing Sandy and Dee Adcock, who adored the historic character of their Colonial Revival home but were less than captivated by the antiquated layout of its kitchen. Built during the Depression in rural Pennsylvania, it had been designed for a household where servants did the cooking and the owners rarely ventured in.

The Adcocks spend more time in the kitchen than anywhere else in the house and they entertain frequently, so their new kitchen had to be as functional as it would be beautiful, within the limits of their budget. Sandy, who had lived with her cramped kitchen for 16 years, was quickly steeped in the project, acting as her own kitchen designer and working alongside an architect.

Small but Efficient

To help them with their plan for the updated kitchen, Sandy and Dee hired architect Joseph Augustine of JFA Architecture in Wyncote,

BEFORE

The inconvenience of a tiny and inefficient kitchen was compounded by the out-of-date look of the original.

AFTER

This kitchen is a seamless integration of old and new, thanks to inspired details. The modern side-by-side refrigerator is covered with panels that match the cabinet design, giving it a traditional, built-in appearance, and the antique furniture reflects the home's Colonial Revival style.

Making It Happen

ESSENTIAL STEP

Sandy wanted a kitchen that blended with the Colonial style of her home, so she was careful about how finish details would flesh out the kitchen's look and functionality. For example, she designed low wainscoting around the breakfast nook because she wanted an upscale, up-to-date feeling. Too much of the paneling would create a farmhouse look. And by showing more of the painted wall, she was able to bring fresh color into the room. In addition, she reused some of the original cabinets, designed the new cabinets in a similar style, and changed the solid mudroom door to a glass French door to echo the glass-fronted cabinets and appear more up to date. All of these details unify the kitchen with the rest of the house.

Pennsylvania. Together Augustine and Sandy revamped the layout, making the space roomier and more livable. Specifically, they eliminated the wall between the kitchen and an adjacent butler's pantry to create a larger, more efficiently organized, family-friendly space. A doorway into the front hall that was the servants' access to the front door was also closed off and replaced with cabinets and counter space, plus an appliance garage.

Although the total floor area of the two rooms has not increased, the more intelligently organized space has additional elbow room. It is now easier for two or three people to move around and cook. Instead of a stove wedged into a corner with virtually no preparation area, Sandy has a centrally

above The stove had to be moved out 4 in. to accommodate a vent pipe behind the wall, but the change proved to be an asset for the homeowner by inadvertently allowing her better access to the back burners.

facing page As a nod to tradition and to maintain a certain formality in the dining room, the original swinging door between the two rooms was retained, although the owners keep it open most of the time.

storage seating

■ Because Sandy believed that it was important that the new kitchen be "people friendly," she welcomed the idea of an in-kitchen eating area. In this nook, family members can enjoy breakfast or supper together, and guests can sit at the table and chat while Sandy cooks. Still, the breakfast nook put great demands on the kitchen's limited space. Architect Joseph Augustine resolved this by designing storage spaces within the bench and fitting it with a hatch and a discreet side drawer. The

whole corner around the bench, with its wainscoting, hanging glass lantern, and antique table and stool, also becomes an important style element within the kitchen, creating a cozy traditional space that invites people in and helps tie the kitchen to the history of the rest of the house.

above Key to remodeling this kitchen was maintaining a high level of utility while adding to the overall beauty of the space, which is open to the living and dining room areas.

situated oven and cooktop with ample counter space on either side for cutting and measuring.

The new cooktop area also sits 4 in. out from the face of the cabinets, a design trick originally employed to make space for a vent duct in the wall behind the oven but which also makes it easier for Sandy to reach the back burners. Plus, because the design is so economical, she was also able to squeeze in extra features such as a new built-in breakfast bench, a table, and a small desk—all without compromising the basic goal of roominess.

quickfixes

When redesigning a vintage kitchen, consider mixing antiques—chairs, light fixtures, even historic artwork—with state-of-the-art appliances to give your kitchen a feeling of richness and authority.

Creative Storage Solutions

Since dismantling the butler's pantry meant losing cabinet space (to create living space), the new plan included some inventive storage solutions. In addition to the small cabinets added to the corner where the former front hall doorway was, architect Augustine designed deep storage spaces into the seats of the new breakfast bench where seldom-used items and appliances are stowed. An old broom closet in the remaining wall of the butler's pantry was reconfigured into an efficient pantry closet, and finally, a shallow pantry closet was created. As a further gesture to efficiency, Sandy tossed out dozens of kitchen items that, on reflection, she decided she didn't need, a simple act that proved to be one key to making her redesign work.

To create a connection between the new kitchen and the historic style of the house, Sandy made a point of reusing specific aspects of the original 1930s kitchen and bypassing the less elegant redecorating touches that had been added in the intervening decades, such as the red plastic-laminate counters and backsplash. She found her inspiration for the look of the new kitchen in the old white glass-door cupboards that were in the

FROM OUR WISH LIST

the kitchen desk

■ The number one item Sandy wanted in her new kitchen was a desk. To fulfill her wish, Augustine designed this pocket-sized desk nestled in between the refrigerator and the dining-room door. At a spare 30 in. across, it is just big enough to file recipes, pay bills, and keep the family on schedule. A set of small cubbies at the bottom of the wall cabinet above serves as storage for mail and stationery, while a nest of drawers to one side includes a deep file drawer for bills and magazine clippings. The desktop is made of stained cherry to match the buffet counter under the old glass cabinets and the dark cherry of the breakfast table.

This early 20th-century kitchen, with its small work area and minimal counter space, couldn't accommodate the needs of a busy family. The Adcocks squeezed living space and extra features into the same area as the old kitchen and butler's pantry.

before&after

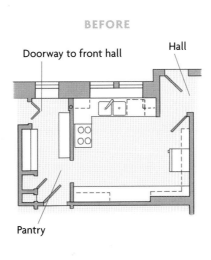

BEFORE

Doorway to front hall
Hall
Pantry

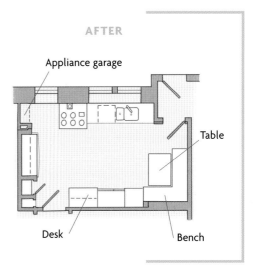

AFTER

Appliance garage
Table
Desk
Bench

butler's pantry, which she later had restored. She also added oak floors that match the rest of the house.

But you would never mistake this kitchen for a 1930s throwback. Sandy intentionally chose a stainless-steel stove, microwave, and dishwasher and flooded the room with bright light from an array of recessed canisters to create contemporary accents, while maintaining the overall feel of a cozy country kitchen.

upclose

above To add storage to the new kitchen, this shallow pantry closet was created along a wall of the mudroom, making good use of otherwise wasted space.

the original cabinetry is all that remains of the old butler's pantry, while the wall that shut it off from the kitchen has given way to a new, more user-friendly plan.

1 A little research into the original oak flooring and varnish color along with some skilled craftsmanship paid off in matching the old floor with the new.

2 Contemporary stainless-steel appliances balance this traditional kitchen.

3 A former passageway to the front hall was closed off and replaced with more useful counter space and an appliance garage.

1 Wood
flooring

2 Stainless-steel
appliances

3 Appliance
garage

"A kitchen designed around sliding doors that went nowhere"

A chic, integrated space chock full of detail

WHEN BART AND SUSAN MOORE DECIDED to redo the kitchen of their townhouse in downtown Houston, they had a pretty clear idea about what was wrong with it. The original 1974 kitchen had a 6-ft.-wide pair of sliding doors along one wall that not only consumed a big chunk of the room's usable wall space but also led to a not terribly useful—and decidedly unattractive—courtyard. The location of the doors meant that the entire work area of the kitchen was confined to a single island with no other counter space except for a narrow 16-in.-wide ledge along one wall that was just big enough to hold a microwave and a few canisters.

In addition to renovating the kitchen, the Moores also wanted to expand the adjacent breakfast area by moving out one exterior wall at the far end of the space by 10 ft. and turning the new space into a family/dining room. They asked Houston architect Virginia Kelsey to create an efficient layout for the entire space and to upgrade the kitchen itself with new cabinets, appliances, and especially unique details. The one

AFTER

The new kitchen resolved nagging layout problems by substituting a wide peninsula for a space-consuming island, and counters and a large window for unattractive sliding doors.

BEFORE

The old kitchen devoted a large amount of valuable counter and floor space just to accommodate this relatively useless pair of sliding doors.

Making It Happen

Architect Virginia Kelsey specified job-built cabinets that were built on site, then had semicustom doors attached. This is a savvy way of producing cabinets with custom fit and features without spending the money custom-built cabinets can cost. First, a cabinetmaker or less expensive finish carpenter builds the boxes and face frames for the cabinets (known as carcases) right in the kitchen. This makes it possible to create perfectly sized cabinets that don't require the many filler strips and shims used with factory-built cabinets. It also allows for exact fit. In the Moores' kitchen, the cabinets along the long wall are 27 in. deep instead of the standard 24 in. to accommodate the cooktop.

proviso that they gave her was to keep a pair of pantry closets that had helped make their original kitchen workable.

An Island or a Peninsula

With the Moores' list of criteria in hand, architect Kelsey came up with a design that solved many of the couple's problems. First, she agreed that the sliding doors had to go. However, she also wanted them to eliminate the freestanding island, which turned out to be a slightly tougher sell. As popular as islands have become in contemporary kitchen design, Kelsey convinced the Moores that a large peninsula would replace many of the functions of the island and do it without consuming as much floor space.

By getting rid of the island and the narrow ledge, Kelsey was able to create an expansive U-shaped layout that gave the Moores three to four times the counter space that they had had in the original kitchen. In place of the sliding-doors-to-nowhere, Kelsey put in far more useful cabinets and counters and topped them with a picture window that lets in light but obscures most of the view of the unsightly high fence and air conditioners. To make up for the lost island, she designed the outer leg of the U as a 42-in.-wide peninsula with ample space for a sink, dishwasher, and food preparation and included a small breakfast bar that allows the couple or their guests to pull up to the peninsula for a quick snack or cup of coffee.

facing page The wide peninsula replaces all of the washing, storage, and food preparation functions of the old island and includes a comfortable breakfast bar, yet it takes up less floor space in the kitchen than the original island.

above By keeping small appliances like the microwave out of the way, the couple is able to keep the countertops in the main kitchen clutter free.

An Eye-Catching Wall

Along the closed part of the U, Kelsey designed a striking-looking wall of 27-in.-deep cabinets with a cooktop and stainless-steel hood in the middle. Although standard counter depth is 24 in., Kelsey felt the extra 3 in. would create a better fit for the cooktop as well as add additional counter space. She was able to customize these dimensions easily because she had specified site-built cabinets.

For the backsplash behind the cooktop and base cabinets, Kelsey and the Moores found a single sample tile that was glazed in a unique green, a hue they decided was the perfect shade for the kitchen but that was out of production. They had it duplicated by a custom tile maker who hand-glazes small batches of tile to specific colors. It was not a hugely expensive splurge that paid off in the distinctive color of the backsplash that helps define this kitchen.

An Integrated Whole

Beyond the U and the peninsula, the architect created a larger dining area and a warm and comfortable family room, complete with a new pair of sliding doors that open onto a far more usable part of the yard. Because of the choices made in the kitchen, particularly the cherry cabinets and the tile, the whole area works as a beautifully integrated room. So efficient is the new layout that the total amount of space in the kitchen is actually smaller than in the previous one, and yet it appears—and functions—as a roomier and more livable space.

above With an open layout, it's doubly important to make sure adjacent areas work with the renovated space. Here the tile surround of the fireplace is a perfect visual counterpoint to the kitchen's backsplash.

twin pantries

Bart and Susan Moore knew from the outset of their remodeling project that they wanted to keep their two pantries. The close proximity of these pantries to the kitchen allowed them to lay in a large supply of cooking necessities without filling up valuable cabinet and kitchen counter space. The architect improved the pantries by building new shelves and counter spaces and adding electrical outlets for small appliances like the coffee-maker and microwave. As a result, many kitchen necessities can be kept off of the counters in the kitchen but remain within easy reach.

before&after

A poor layout derived from a cookie-cutter design translated into little counter space— save for the island. The design makes far better use of the existing space, which, combined with the family and dining areas, has become the heart of the Moores' home.

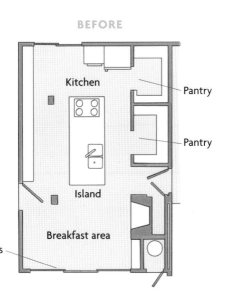

BEFORE

Kitchen

Pantry

Pantry

Island

Breakfast area

Sliding doors

AFTER

Pantry

Kitchen

Pantry

Peninsula

Breakfast area

Family room

upclose

2 Lazy Susan corner cabinet

3 Frosted glass doors

1 Slide-out pot storage rack

by reorganizing the layout of the old kitchen, upgrading the style, and adding lots of savvy storage features, the remodeled kitchen allows the Moores to pack more livability into a smaller area.

1 For ready access to oversized pots and pans, this slide-out storage rack is located beneath the cooktop.

2 This traditional lazy Susan shelf system creates access to an otherwise dead corner in the base cabinets.

3 Frosted glass in the upper cabinet doors creates the elegant appearance of a china cabinet without the cluttered look of a crowded cupboard.

4 The green tiles on the backsplash were hand-glazed to a color specified by the homeowners.

4 Custom tiles

granite honed, not polished

■ The countertops in this kitchen are honed black granite; in other words, they have a matte instead of a polished finish. Honing, which produces a softer, warmer appearance, has become the popular choice for all sorts of stone countertops, replacing the shiny finishes that were common a decade ago. The difference is achieved simply in the coarseness of the abrasives used to grind the surface. If you find a polished stone pattern you like, but want it honed, you can often have it refinished as honed stone before it leaves the stone yard. The chief disadvantage of honed granite is that it is more porous, so it needs to be sealed when new and resealed every two years.

counter choices

KITCHEN COUNTERS MUST BE easy to work on and to clean. They also add almost as much to the look of the kitchen as the cabinets. Here is a quick overview of the most common materials.

GRANITE For natural good looks, durability, and hardness, granite is a top choice. It comes in several finishes: polished (high gloss), honed (matte), and flamed (rough) and in many colors and patterns. However, granite can chip and crack, and is available only in 8-ft. to 10-ft. lengths (longer counters require seams).

SOAPSTONE A popular choice for those who want a warm and traditional stone counter. Like all real stone, soapstone will crack and chip, and must be seamed in long counters.

CAST CONCRETE For those who want the warmth of soapstone in a wider choice of colors, cast concrete is an excellent choice.

QUARTZ COMPOSITE Made of 90 percent to 95 percent quartz powder in an acrylic resin, composite countertops look like real granite but can be installed without seams and can be repaired. Major brands are CaesarStone®, DuPont® Zodiaq®, Cambria® Quartz, Silestone®, and Formica® Stone.

SOLID SURFACE OR ACRYLIC Acrylic counters can be installed without seams, can have custom edge treatments, can be repaired if scratched or burned, and are available in a huge selection of colors.

LAMINATE Durable plastic sheets that are glued to wood or fiberboard substrates, laminate countertops are the least expensive and have the widest choice of colors and patterns.

STAINLESS STEEL Sleek, durable, and easy to maintain, stainless countertops work well and look great in clean, contemporary-style kitchens.

BUTCHER BLOCK This time-tested material works well as a complement to other countertop materials, such as stainless steel or granite.

above This basic natural black stone has a soft, warm appeal.

above Granite is available in a variety of finishes, including this rough-textured "flamed" finish.

above Cast concrete offers the feel of a soft stone counter.

above As restaurant owners have known for years, stainless-steel countertops are sanitary and low-maintenance.

above Quartz composite counters look like stone.

above Acrylic countertops deliver function and style without breaking the bank.

left Classic butcher-block countertops still make perfect sense in today's heavy-use kitchens.

"More work space on the stove than the countertops"

A bright kitchen that looks bigger than it is

NOTHING ABOUT THE DESIGN of this small kitchen worked when Ivo Hug and Kristen Garneau bought it—not the size, not the shape, not the light, and on some days, not even the oven. Squeezed into the back corner of their tiny house in Mill Valley, California, the kitchen was dark, cramped, and falling apart, with low, crumbling ceilings, one small window, a single door, and no storage or work space. Their goal was to clean it up, literally and figuratively, create more cabinet and counter space, and open up the entire area.

Since the house sat on a small lot, the kitchen could not be expanded outward. Similarly, if they allowed the kitchen to move into the rest of the house, the couple would have no living space. It was obvious that whatever they accomplished would have to take place within the existing 9-ft. by 11-ft. footprint of the old kitchen and would have to involve some highly creative reworking of the existing space.

From the start, this was going to be a complete gut-remodeling project, meaning the removal of everything down to the studs. This fact proved to be a bonus

AFTER

The owners and their architect used several sly tricks, including a mirrored wall, high ceiling, and large skylight, to make this tiny kitchen look spacious.

BEFORE

In the beginning, the kitchen was a disaster zone, with few fixtures and lots of water damage.

before & after

The kitchen was filled with a hodgepodge of cabinets and appliances and was completely walled off from the dining area. The simple new design packs storage and counter space into the same floor area. The addition of a breakfast bar opens up the kitchen to the dining room.

BEFORE

Patio

Kitchen

Dining room

AFTER

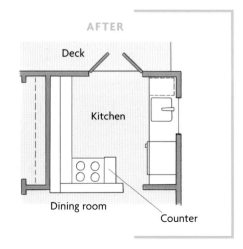

Deck

Kitchen

Dining room

Counter

facing page The mirrored wall not only doubles the apparent space in the kitchen but also amplifies the sunlight that the skylight brings into the room.

because it allowed the couple to start with a proverbial "blank slate."

To help them fill that slate, they hired Sausalito, California-based architect Barry Peterson of Deliberate Design, who devised a plan to open up the kitchen both to the rest of the house as well as to the outside, especially to the new deck they were building. Peterson also came up with ideas to make the kitchen more workable by adding more counter and storage space and ultimately a considerable amount of charm that the room had previously lacked.

Lightening Up

To create more of a visual connection to the rest of the first floor, Peterson knocked down the wall separating the kitchen from the living room and replaced it with a breakfast bar. To bring in the sunny outdoors, a requirement the couple considered essential to the redesign, the narrow doorway to the backyard was widened to make room for a pair of French doors, and the small window over the sink was replaced with a large picture window. The most effective element of the design, however, was the mirrored wall Peterson designed, which created the illusion that the kitchen is far larger than it really is.

That illusion became even more powerful after the couple dealt with the problem of their low ceiling. At the start of the project, the plan had been simply to replace the water-damaged 8-ft. ceiling with new drywall, but when Ivo and Kristen pulled it down and cleaned up the mess, they decided they liked having the kitchen open to the roof. The change necessitated a brief pause

Working with Pros

The couple was clear with the architect and contractor that they were working with a limited budget. To help them save money, the contractor, Phil Kline, worked out ways for them to do many chores themselves—something that not all contractors are comfortable doing. Ivo and Kristen performed the demolition themselves, while Kristen did much of the sanding and painting and Ivo built the deck and trellis. Architect Barry Peterson specified many of the fixtures from suppliers outside of the expensive Bay Area. In rural Northern California, he found a small custom cabinetmaker to create cherry cabinets and shelving, and he tracked down a millwork shop that made windows and doors from redwood that had been recycled from old wine casks.

quickfixes

You can add usable space to any kitchen by annexing outdoor areas and integrating them with dining furniture and, say, herb or kitchen gardens.

space simple

■ Fitting a workable kitchen into the limited space was a necessary challenge for Kristen and Ivo, who love to cook and entertain regularly. They did it by throwing out or storing everything they didn't use regularly and by using every possible nook and cranny for storage, including an appliance bay designed by Kristen around the refrigerator and simple, open shelves for china and glassware. The only space hogs permitted were the professional-quality, 36-in. Dynasty® six-burner gas range and the high-power vent hood. To create work surfaces, the homeowners added stainless-steel countertops and then permitted themselves only one or two appliances.

in the construction to design a new truss system, which would replace the old ceiling joists and support the roof—and a somewhat longer pause while the couple figured out how to pay for the added expense. The result is, visually, a much larger kitchen.

A pleasant side effect of this open-ceiling design was that it allowed Peterson to add a 4-ft. by 6-ft. louvered skylight over the center of the kitchen to bring still more sunlight into the modest space. Combined with the effect of the mirrored wall, the skylight has made the new kitchen an especially bright space, one that is strongly connected to the outdoors.

left The view from the dining room shows off a key design addition to this modest space—the breakfast bar, which replaced a solid wall. By opening up the connection, the homeowners gained even more virtual space.

mirror, mirror

■ The mirrored wall above the long counter is central to the design of this kitchen, adding greatly to the sense of light and space. But getting it right proved to be one of the major challenges of the project. Given the location of the mirror with truss beams intersecting it at 90 degrees, the installation had to be perfectly plumb and flat. Otherwise, the reflected beams would appear bent or distorted. To accomplish this, the contractor covered the wall with smooth plywood, leveling everything as he went. The mirror was then precisely cut and fitted around the beams and carefully glued on to the plywood with an even spread of adhesive. Also, by installing the mirror above eye level, the couple gained all of the benefits of a mirror without the irritations, such as constantly seeing themselves moving around the room.

Outdoor Extensions

The new deck with a dining table located just steps from the French doors serves as an active extension of the new kitchen for much of the year, especially since just beyond the deck are an outdoor cooking area and an herb garden. An elaborate overhead trellis covers the deck. Eventually, fast-growing wisteria vines will fill in this structure, but in the meantime Kristen has artfully woven canvas strips through the cross members to mute the sunlight.

Although they couldn't add real space to their small kitchen, Ivo and Kristen have found a number of creative ways to borrow visual and physical space from the areas around it, making it functionally much larger and lighter. What's more, it has allowed them to inhabit their entire living space—both indoors and out—more completely.

above With balmy California weather just out their back door, the couple designed their deck to be part of the kitchen by adding furniture and an arbor with a canvas awning.

upclose

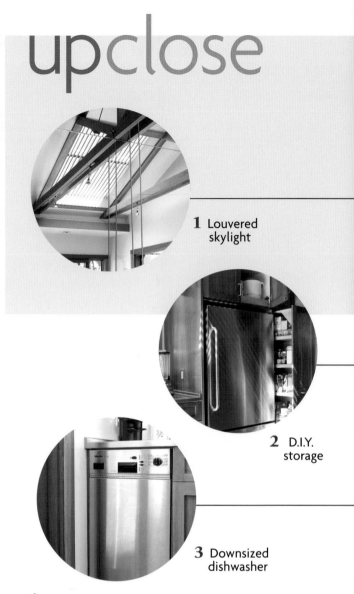

1 Louvered skylight

2 D.I.Y. storage

3 Downsized dishwasher

The new kitchen is a study in economy. Light, open space, and smart cabinet design make every square inch usable.

1 A large skylight is covered with simple, fixed louvers to minimize the heat gain from the midday sun.

2 The homeowners designed a pull-out pantry and appliance cabinet to fit snugly around their refrigerator.

3 To save space in this tightly organized kitchen, the couple chose an 18-in. dishwasher in lieu of a standard 24-in. size.

"Love the Craftsman style; hate the cramped space"

THE SOLUTION

A modern bungalow kitchen with echoes of its past

AFTER

This kitchen was designed to reflect the Craftsman style of the house yet provide the owners with much-needed space. The center table gives the kitchen an old-fashioned warmth that is also reflected in the apron sink and painted cabinetry.

REATING A NEW KITCHEN in an old house requires striking a balance between honoring the style and character of the original and responding to the modern need for space, storage, and convenience. Greg and Sundari Mase were the owners of just such a home with elements of Spanish Revival and Craftsman styles. Their charming but tired kitchen had hardly been touched since the house was built in Kensington, California, in 1925, and was squeezed into a maze of small rooms that limited both its beauty and its function.

In replacing this kitchen, the Mases hoped to preserve as much of its original—but long-lost—appeal as possible, while updating it. They also wanted to keep the new kitchen more or less within the footprint of the old yet integrate it with adjacent rooms to create a wide-open space. They saw this new kitchen/dining/family room as a single gathering place where they could keep tabs on their three young children, visit with friends while cooking, and maximize their great views of San Francisco Bay.

BEFORE

Although the original kitchen was claustrophobic and worn out, the Mases found the authentically old-fashioned face-frame cabinetry charming and wanted this sort of detail reflected in the new kitchen.

Working with Pros

Viewing the actual work of a prospective architect or designer is a great way to find one whose style agrees with yours. Getting access to an architect's work, however, is not always easy. The Mases found a great solution by signing up for a kitchen tour sponsored by a local charity. Out of this process they discovered Berkeley architect Jim Miller, who frequently worked in the Craftsman style that they wanted but who also took it a step further. He not only chose historically appropriate details and materials but also encouraged contractors wherever feasible to use such traditional methods as on-site cabinet construction and old-fashioned finishes. Finding an architect who shared their sense of style saved the Mases time and stress, critical factors in any kitchen renovation.

On a benefit kitchen tour in nearby Berkeley, they found architect Jim Miller, who had a passion for the type of classical Craftsman-style kitchen the Mases hoped to create. Together they came up with a plan that accomplished the Mases' goals in a way that would be consistent with the style of the house.

Honoring Craftsmanship

The reorganized space that Miller designed includes dedicated cooking, dining, and gathering areas that are all connected to one another and, thanks to a wall of windows and French doors, all share the view. The kitchen keeps the simple L-shaped cabinet layout of the old but now wraps around an ample farm-style table that provides additional work and entertaining space. A modest 1-ft.-deep bump-out was engineered into the exterior wall behind the sink to add slightly to the space.

To remain true to the traditional character of the original kitchen, Miller designed face-frame cabinets with fitted, inset doors and drawers, which require more careful craftsmanship because all of the pieces must fit together flawlessly. The cabinets were built mostly on site, which is how it was done at the turn of the 20th century. They also were painted with brushed-on alkyd enamel paint because the Mases wanted the small brushstrokes that express the handcrafted nature of the cabinets to be visible. (Today most cabinet finishes are sprayed on and baked at the factory.) Miller also designed the cabinets with faux furniture-style legs to give them a more old-fashioned appearance.

above The cast concrete countertops and backsplash are stylish counterpoints to the reproduction pendant lamp and simple custom cabinetry that keep faith with this Craftsman makeover.

One element in the kitchen that departs significantly from tradition is the cast concrete that Miller chose for the counters and stove backsplash. Although at first glance it might seem that concrete would be too hard and too modern a material for the space, concrete actually mimics the warmth and softness of traditional soapstone countertops and can be colored to match the cabinets.

cast concrete

■ Although the countertops appear old-fashioned, they (and the backsplash) are made of a popular material in kitchen design, cast concrete. Concrete creates a warmer and softer

surface than a stone such as granite but resists heat and cracking and is structurally stronger. Many users also like the subtle variations in color and texture that occur in casting each piece and the patina that is acquired if the countertops are left unsealed. Other big advantages are that it can be dyed to virtually any color and molded into most shapes. It is generally less expensive than stone, although not by much. Concrete should be sealed about once a year if you want to avoid stains.

Warming Up Space

To replace the bearing walls that were demolished and to create the open space that also defines this new kitchen, an engineered-lumber beam was installed in the ceiling. Oak floors were used throughout, including in the kitchen, to enhance the sense of spaciousness to tie the kitchen visually to the larger space and to add to the room's vintage charm.

Understanding that open rooms can sometimes feel impersonal, Miller divided it with a stairwell that connects the family room/kitchen with a basement playroom. Next to the stairwell, Miller positioned a low island containing a bookcase and cabinets. By placing the stairwell and island in this location, he was able to separate the cooking and eating side of the space from the family room side, making each designated area more discreet and friendly but without sacrificing the overall spaciousness and light. To tame the area further, Miller used Douglas fir for the windows and doors around the edge of the room and in the stairwell banister and bookshelf. The honey-colored wood warms up the room and unifies it at the same time.

It's never easy to redesign an old room to do justice to its history yet satisfy contemporary needs. And that goes double for a kitchen. But with equal parts architectural savvy and creative use of details, the Mases have succeeded with this kitchen—and have done so beautifully.

facing page The central bookcase helps to disguise and dress up the stairway, adds needed storage, and creates a visual boundary between the kitchen and the new family room.

left This drop-down sink underlines the traditional feel of the kitchen.

The old layout of the Mases' kitchen included lots of doors and walls and a stairway hall placed smack in the middle of the view. By opening up the walls and adding a small bump-out, the Mases gained a great deal of usable living area without resorting to major reconstruction.

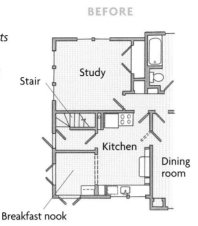

BEFORE

Stair

Study

Kitchen

Dining room

Breakfast nook

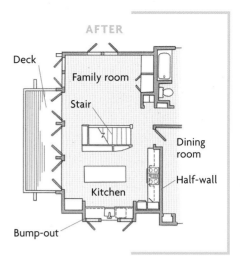

AFTER

Deck

Family room

Stair

Dining room

Kitchen

Half-wall

Bump-out

ADDED INGREDIENTS

from the farmhouse

■ The Mases' kitchen cabinets were designed with "furniture-style legs," one of the most popular trends in kitchen design today. The "unfitted" cabinet look comes from traditional English farm kitchens, where movable pieces of furniture are the custom, and provides a country-style alternative to the ubiquitous built-in or "fitted" cabinets. The problem with true unfitted cabinets, though, is that the narrow, open spaces beneath them collect dust and dirt and are difficult to clean. One solution is to keep a recessed toe-kick in place behind the furniture-style legs to prevent a buildup of dirt and to add to the strength of the cabinet.

quickfixes

Tours of recently renovated or redecorated houses are a great way to see the work of several prospective architects and designers at once. Check local newspapers for upcoming tours.

upclose

1 Decorative cutout

although this kitchen is state of the art, it has an old-fashioned feeling to it, thanks to such elements as the nicely detailed cabinetry and the furniture-style legs.

1 A decorative cutout was used to support small spice shelves on either side of the range and to add to the traditional appeal of the design.

2 The architect created a mini-hutch in a tight area by clustering drawers and cabinets into what would otherwise be an underused corner countertop.

3 The curved bookcase by the stair well, perfect for shelving frequently used cookbooks, began as a stylistic touch but works to ease traffic flow and stop painful bumps that can occur with a squared-off corner.

2 Fitted cupboards and shelves

3 Curvy cabinetry

"No room for her in the bachelor-pad kitchen"

THE SOLUTION

Efficiency + comfort = domestic bliss

AS ANY BACHELOR WILL TELL YOU, a kitchen with a working microwave and a cold refrigerator is usually all he needs. Add a sophisticated—albeit a bit more traditional—wife to the mix and the requirements change. Here, the sum total of this sort of personal math is a gracious kitchen that retains its contemporary style and organization but has been upgraded with new equipment, charming structural and utilitarian details, and a large dollop of, dare we say, feminine warmth.

The evolution of this compromise began 10 years ago when the owner, then a single man, bought this 1980s house in Southampton, New York. At first, he left the kitchen as he found it, a contemporary bachelor pad with a simple, workable space, where the most important culinary challenges were worked out over the phone, ordering in take-out food. That all changed when he got married five years ago. Redoing the old kitchen quickly rose to the top of the couple's to-do list, but it had to be renovated in a way that honored both his wish to maintain the kitchen's

AFTER

Although this kitchen occupies exactly the same space as the old one, it has been entirely transformed by the fresh design and visually rich wood and stainless finishes used in the renovation.

BEFORE

The white-on-white plastic laminate décor of the former kitchen served the minimal purposes of a bachelor, but the look seemed dated and cold to his new wife.

Finding Your Style

The happy marriage of diverse styles that went into this kitchen results from the creative use of finishing details. Although the overall sensibility of the design is contemporary, much of it is rendered in natural, "soft" materials such as the mahogany in the columns, windows, and doors and the maple for the cabinets, giving the space a more traditional look. The cleft-slate floor tiles, the flamed granite countertops, the highly crafted island, and the built-in, cabinet-style refrigerator and dishwasher add to the sense of warmth. At the same time, such details as the stainless steel on the island, backsplash, range, and hood; the spare cabinets with their flat, full-overlay door design; and the edgy pendant lamps over the island recenter the design on its contemporary origins.

above Natural materials such as maple cabinets, granite counters, and redwood window trim have replaced the all-laminate-all-the-time look of the old kitchen, creating warmth and comfort.

open, efficient feel and her desire to add warmth and texture. He saw a clean, industrial-style, low-maintenance space. She saw a softer, more traditional kitchen, layered with a lot of wood and details.

Marrying Two Styles

The synthesis of these two visions was worked out by architect Erica Broberg. She kept the simple, square shape of the original but added a small island in the middle and updated the existing breakfast bar, bringing in some sleek metal stools that play off the kitchen's new stainless-steel elements. She also opened up the walls around the kitchen so that it would communicate more easily with the adjoining spaces. Views and traffic flow between the modest-sized kitchen and the large, open dining/living space were

above The cabinets and hood over the range are suspended from the ceiling to allow for an opening toward the front of the house, thus reducing the closed-in feel of the kitchen and adding new sight lines.

maintained, while new access was opened up toward the front of the house and the workout room the couple created there. This borrowing of visual space from the surrounding rooms has made the formerly cramped-feeling kitchen seem far larger and created the look of a loftlike space that the husband wanted. At the same time, the sense of spaciousness allowed the kitchen itself to feel more welcoming, a strong wish of the wife's.

To enhance the spare, low-maintenance efficiency of the original plan and to keep the look contemporary, Broberg included lots of high-tech

above By keeping the size of the island down to the bare minimum, the new design leaves plenty of room for two people to move around in this not-too-large kitchen.

before & after

The layout of the old kitchen allowed only one way in and one way out, making it both inconvenient and claustrophobic-feeling. A couple of minor design tweaks, such as creating a small opening in one corner and adding a compact island, have made the new kitchen far more user-friendly.

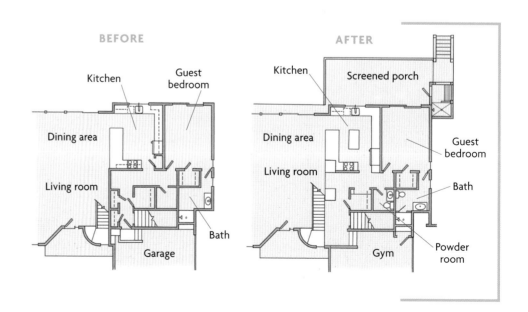

BEFORE

Kitchen

Guest bedroom

Dining area

Living room

Bath

Garage

AFTER

Kitchen

Screened porch

Dining area

Living room

Guest bedroom

Bath

Gym

Powder room

stainless steel in the form of the range, hood, backsplashes, and the top of the island. Stainless steel is sanitary, durable, waterproof, heat resistant, and easy to clean—the ideal material for a kitchen surface—but it can be tricky when applied on countertops and backsplashes as it is here, since even tiny imperfections will eventually show up as bumps in the stainless. All of these pieces were fabricated off site out of 14-gauge steel and installed over a smooth subsurface to ensure a flat installation.

To add a touch of tradition, Broberg also dressed up the design with richer materials and layers of detail. Custom-crafted maple cabinets with simple, flat doors replaced the charmless white laminate cabinets of the original. A column clad in dark mahogany creates a dramatic sculptural anchor at one corner of the new design, while it adds warmth to the overall space. She used flamed black granite for the countertops around the outside of the square. The flaming process leaves the surface of the stone slightly

cabinet chic

■ While the two columns flanking the hallway outside the kitchen help define the new space, the architect saw that they could do more than merely serve as architectural showpieces. She turned the hollow interior of one of the columns, which was conveniently located near both the kitchen and the dining area, into a stylish storage cabinet for china and glassware. The glass door to the cabinet faces into the hallway and away from the living space so that the clean, structural appearance of the column is maintained when viewed from the  living room. Glass shelves and a pair of halogen puck lights make the display items within both beautiful and easy to find.

left A pair of large, mahogany-clad columns visually anchors the design of the new kitchen but is cleverly designed with hidden cabinets that add function.

rough, giving it a seemingly old-fashioned, hand-tooled finish. Together, the dark wood column and the flamed black granite countertops bring the weight of craftsmanship to the largely machine-made environment, adding textures.

Complexity without Clutter

The thoughtful mixing of materials—the use of steel on the island top and stone on the counter-tops and the dark and light woods—also creates complexity and visual interest without producing a sense of clutter. The result of this careful blend of hard and soft, cool and warm, space and detail is a sophisticated kitchen that is as inviting as it is efficient and as comfortable as it is chic.

above The broad horizontal window above the kitchen sink was designed to double as a convenient pass-through to the dining area on the porch just outside.

1 Flamed granite counters

this little kitchen packs in a lot of both form and function by using savvy style and storage tricks.

1 To give the black granite counters a warmer and more sensual appeal, the designer chose flame-treated granite, which has a highly tactile surface.

2 To protect the easily scratchable stain-less steel, a butcher-block cutting board was inserted into the countertop on the island. It can be traded for a marble insert for rolling out pastry.

3 This vertical tray cupboard by the sink keeps trays, platters, and baking sheets out of sight.

4 Making use of every space, like this storage area above the refrigerator, is key to keeping the counters uncluttered.

2 Butcher-block
insert

3 Vertical
tray storage

4 Storage above
refrigerator

above Laminate finishes add easy-to-maintain convenience and contemporary flair to a modern-style kitchen but don't work with more traditional designs.

cabinet council

HE TYPE AND STYLE OF CABINETS you select will define the look and feel of your new kitchen more than any other single choice you make. They may also account for the largest percentage of the total cost of your project, so you need to make smart choices.

To decide which cabinets you want, you need to understand the basic variables of cabinet construction and how these choices affect cost and style. The three basic questions to consider are:

1. FACE FRAME OR FRAMELESS? Kitchen cabinets come in two basic configurations: face frame and frameless. Face-frame construction uses a 2-in.- to 3-in.-wide frame around the opening of each cabinet, which is a less expensive way of adding strength but also reduces the usable width of the opening by 3 in. to 4 in. Many better cabinets use frameless construction, which allows full access to the entire width of the cabinet.

2. INSET OR OVERLAY? Cabinet doors and drawers are available in overlay or inset designs. Overlay doors and drawers cover the frames around the openings and mimic frameless cabinets in appearance. Inset designs are crafted to sit inside the opening of the frame and are generally more expensive.

3. TRADITIONAL OR CONTEMPORARY? Generally speaking, traditional cabinets are built with frame construction and inset doors and drawers, while contemporary-style cabinets almost always feature overlay doors and drawers. However,

left Traditional-style doors and drawers can be used in a full overlay configuration on frameless cabinets to mix the look of the old with the efficiency of the new.

left Cabinets built in a traditional manner feature frame construction with doors and drawers fitted or inset into the framed openings of the cabinet fronts. Painted finishes also give these cabinets a vintage appearance.

traditional-style overlay doors and drawers will cost less than fitted inset styles.

Styles and Finishes

Most building centers and kitchen showrooms offer an array of door styles, finishes, and wood species. The choices are virtually infinite, especially when you add painted, baked-on, or laminate finishes to the myriad stains and varnishes. Be sure to carefully research the mix that best suits you and your kitchen.

Before you buy factory-manufactured stock, semicustom, or "custom" cabinets (some manufacturers offer what they call "custom" design service, which is usually very limited, that is, not custom), it pays to explore the possibility of using cabinets that are truly custom built by local craftsmen. Because you will be avoiding the shipping costs, sales commissions, and markups that go with factory-built, store-bought cabinets, you may be able to buy something built exactly to your needs for little more cost.

above Flat cabinet fronts with full overlay doors and drawers are used in most contemporary kitchens where spare, unadorned surfaces are the goal. The natural maple finished in clear varnish adds to the effect.

"A weekend builder's prefab delight"

A beautifully crafted kitchen for a family of six

WHEN MAUREEN AND KEVIN MIRABILE bought this early-'80s contemporary house in Montauk, Long Island, they knew they had a problem: The front door opened right into the kitchen. And this wasn't just any old kitchen; this was a prefabricated nightmare, a 20-year-old space covered with yellowing white and wood-grained laminate. The fact that the house was in a great location and possessed a pleasant, laid-back ambiance made it a perfect choice for this active family of six. And possibly because of that unfortunate door, the Mirabiles figured they were free to create the gorgeous kitchen they really wanted, especially for Maureen, who, as a devoted mom—and a devoted cook—spent a tremendous amount of time there.

It was no surprise that when the Mirabiles got down to planning their dream kitchen with Long Island architect Erica Broberg, the first order of business was that problematic layout. The new kitchen, they decided, should stay in the same place but be reoriented 90 degrees so that it opened into the existing living/dining area.

BEFORE

The homeowners' original kitchen was not only tiny, inconvenient (with the front door opening into its midst), and tired, but was virtually unusable for a large family.

AFTER

The fix for the original prefab galley kitchen is a stylish and roomy U-shaped space that is packed with charm and ready to take on the needs of an active family.

Defining Your Space

Coming up with a new layout for the high-traffic, family-friendly kitchen was the number one priority for the Mirabiles. The intrusive front door had to go, which would allow them to claim that wall space for cabinets and counters. In place of the closed counter-and-peninsula configuration, the architect designed a U-shaped kitchen that welcomes like a pair of open arms and positioned an expansive island in the middle to separate the working kitchen from the family dining area. Plenty of storage cabinets and working counter space is included in the central U as well as in the large center island.

The area where the former front door had been became a counter and cabinet space with a new window that caught the morning sun. The adjoining living and dining areas also stayed where they had originally been, but now the two spaces were blended seamlessly into each other. The whole area became a wide-open, multipurpose living/dining space with the kitchen as its most integral part. To anchor the scheme, Broberg chose a classic, symmetrical composition for the new kitchen, created by wrapping the cabinets and appliances in a large U around a dark, furniture-style island.

Practical, Beautiful Details

Maureen's primary request was that the kitchen be both functional and beautiful. As a stay-at-home mother with four kids, she would be demanding a lot from her kitchen. She understood that such a well-organized space, especially

one with its own great look, would make her life easier.

Broberg addressed Maureen's wishes for both practicality and good looks by coming up with an artful mix of elements and details, especially in the cabinetry, and frequently contrasting the old with the new, the traditional with the modern.

The architect chose semicustom cabinets, which allowed her to pick from a menu of features that would not be available with stock factory-built cabinets and to create a few details of her own. For example, she used traditional

above The new kitchen is intimately connected to the dining and living rooms—great for watching kids while you cook—but it's also enclosed and separate enough to work with little intrusion.

facing page The high-heat, pro-style range was placed in the deepest part of the U, safely away from child-friendly areas like the dining table and drink cooler.

ADDED INGREDIENTS

drinks all around

■ The under-the-counter beverage center located at the end of the U nearest the living room allows the Mirabiles' kids to quickly grab a cool drink without entering the kitchen or opening the refrigerator. The cooler is essentially identical to the typical

under-the-counter wine chillers on the market, except that it has a different configuration of shelves, designed to accommodate dozens of soda (or beer) cans. It also includes two wooden slide-out racks that can handle either cans or a few bottles of wine, and it can be refitted with wine shelves when the kids leave for college.

face-frame cabinets with flush drawers and doors to evoke solid, old-fashioned craftsmanship. These were painted with a rich, custom-mixed cream-colored finish, which was factory applied and baked on, giving the cabinets a clean and sophisticated but timeless presence. Broberg designed a unique pair of small, hutch-style drawer cabinets above the counter on either end of the range wall to add a touch of Arts and Crafts style and make creative use of otherwise wasted space. Other details, such as the white apron sink, retro-style nickel cabinet hardware, and the furniture-style cherry island, point to a fondness for old-time good looks.

Contemporary Comfort

Although Broberg and the Mirabiles wanted beautiful traditional details, they also wanted a few gorgeous contemporary elements to give life to the kitchen and surrounding living/dining space. The black granite countertops plus the large stainless-steel range and refrigerator balance the kitchen's style with modern accents. The tall, sculptural vent hood that reaches up to the high ceiling centers the entire space.

before & after

Very little space was apportioned for the kitchen in this builder home. Adding the island and half-wall created a U-shaped kitchen that remained connected to the dining and living areas.

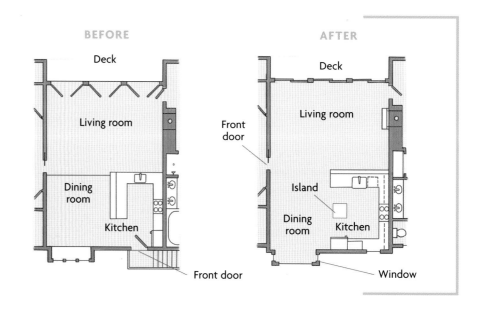

quickfixes

Woven baskets for storage add charm to a traditional kitchen. For a more contemporary look, you can use wire baskets or colorful plastic containers.

above Antique-style touches like the apron-front sink and old-fashioned faucet give this kitchen a classic feel.

left This kitchen is a delightfully eclectic mix of the traditional with the modern. The face-frame cabinets, hutch-style drawers, and old-fashioned nickel hardware contrast with the trendy hard-wood floor and the stainless-steel appliances.

Ultimately, this is an active kitchen designed for a big family. This is evident in such well-thought-out features as a beverage center at one end of the U so the kids can quickly grab a can of soda, the warming drawers that ease the task of creating big meals, and the bottom-mount refrigerator that makes access to frozen snacks easy. This kitchen not only mixes finishes and styles but also blends classic comfort and ease with a contemporary sensibility for the best of both worlds.

upclose

loving island living

■ The large island in the center of the kitchen functions both as the visual anchor as well as the organizational center for most of the food preparation. Produced by the same shop that did the other cabinets and made of the same cherry but stained a dark cherry color, the island is designed to stand as a piece apart. Instead of using the same granite as the countertops, the island is topped with traditional-style butcher block, not only for practical reasons, since it is an ideal surface for food preparation, but also for stylistic reasons, since it further defines the island as a stand-alone piece. Furniture-style legs and finished end panels help to enhance this distinction. Open shelves with woven storage baskets add a casual touch to the otherwise somewhat streamlined design.

1 Hide-away dishwasher

Unique design features such as the dark-stained island and the wall-cabinet doors that are glazed on the bottom and solid on the top contribute to the individuality of this kitchen.

1 To maintain the clean visual line of cream-colored cabinets around the outside U, the dishwasher is disguised with a false door-and-drawer front.

2 A half-moon rack, used to store items in a blind corner of the cabinets, swings out in a more efficient way than traditional lazy Susan carousels.

3 A drawer that keeps food warm while other dishes are being prepared is always helpful when feeding a crowd.

4 Pull-out shelves allow for easy access to large and heavy objects, such as pots, pans, platters, and bowls.

2 Swing-out
storage rack

3 Warming
drawer

4 Pull-out
cabinet shelves

"An almost original kitchen, unfortunately"

A Victorian-style kitchen with inspired improvements

WHEN JENNIFER AND CHRIS BEAN bought this Victorian house near downtown Montpelier, Vermont, in 1999, it had been owned by the same family for more than 100 years. In all that time, virtually nothing had been altered. For example, the existing kitchen was little more than an empty room with a refrigerator and a stove. Although the space included a large butler's pantry, it was effectively sealed off from the kitchen by a heavy door that made it inconvenient to use. An adjacent mudroom offered storage space but not much else.

The Beans embarked on an ambitious, two-pronged plan to renovate their kitchen. Like many owners of old houses, they loved the Victorian character and the details that had attracted them to the house in the first place, yet they weren't interested in living in a museum. But their new kitchen had to be rugged enough to handle their family lifestyle. Plus, they wanted modern appliances and other contemporary features—like a breakfast bar—that would have been out of place in the kitchen 100 years ago. The Beans decided to

BEFORE

The former butler's pantry was well equipped by the standards of 1900, but needed to be updated.

AFTER

With this Victorian-style kitchen, the Beans got exactly what they wanted: a spacious, modern kitchen with 19th-century-style cabinetry and detail.

Defining Your Space

The Beans' house was built in a time when the kitchen was a working space for cooks or busy housewives, not a gathering space for family and certainly not for guests. True to its historic standard, the original kitchen here was placed at the back of the house adjacent to the pantry and the mudroom. To get the space they needed, the Beans moved the main working kitchen into the space the mudroom once occupied and combined it with a piece of the old kitchen. The updated butler's pantry now opens up into the new, larger kitchen. All that remains of the walls that separated the three rooms is a supporting steel column (now clad in oak to match the cabinets) that carries the weight of the former wall.

above New cabinets were hand-built on-site to reproduce the details of the original kitchen and to fit the unique angles of the old space.

combine the original kitchen with the unfinished mudroom and the fully finished butler's pantry. This open plan, perhaps the biggest departure from tradition, works beautifully.

Designing with Wood

The Beans' original Victorian butler's pantry was a handsome piece of built-in furniture. The cupboards and shelving were utterly authentic, created with quartersawn oak (wood sawn around the outside of the heart of the tree that yields an especially tight vertical grain), which, in fact, had been used for most of the original woodwork throughout the kitchen. However, the shelves in the pantry were designed to hold delicate cups and saucers and small canisters, items typical of the era. Not a single shelf was tall enough to handle a standard-size cereal box.

left The mix of old and new, of authentic details and stainless-steel appliances, and of soapstone counters and a laminate-covered peninsula give this kitchen its charm.

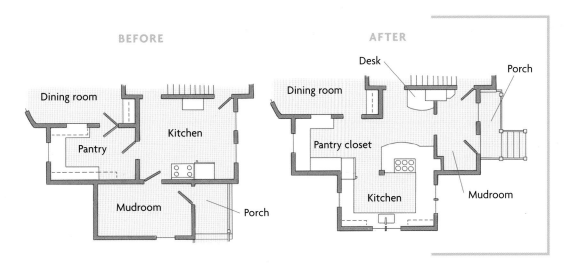

before & after

In the old plan, the kitchen, pantry, and mudroom were walled off from each other and the rest of the house. The kitchen has been moved and expanded and is now connected to the pantry and the front hall.

BEFORE

Dining room

Pantry

Kitchen

Mudroom

Porch

AFTER

Desk

Porch

Dining room

Pantry closet

Kitchen

Mudroom

pantry pride

■ Architect Irene Facciolo redesigned the butler's pantry using the same materials and details but increased the dimensions of the shelves. Within the floor-to-ceiling pantry cabinet, tightly spaced shelves designed for tea services and small containers were rebuilt to handle the supersize boxes and cans that end up in most kitchens today. Handy roll-out shelves were added. The original upper cabinets were situated too close to the lower base cabinets, making the counters dark and hard to use. The architect raised the upper cabinets to create space and light and added under-cabinet lights and outlets to accommodate small electrical appliances. The pantry was also opened up to the rest of the kitchen, making it far more user-friendly.

quickfixes

Because soapstone oxidizes to a darker color when exposed to water or oil, it should be treated with mineral oil when first installed, then each year after that to produce a uniform oxidation.

above A cooktop is set into the peninsula while an under-the-counter oven is located a few feet away allowing one person to bake while another sautées.

To extend the elegant woodwork of the butler's pantry into the adjoining new spaces, the Beans' architect, Irene Facciolo of Thunder Mill Design, created new cabinets and trim using the same oak wood and had molding cut to match the patterns of the surviving cabinetry. To remain true to the historic spirit of the kitchen, the Beans decided to have the cabinets made as they would have been 100 years ago—on site—even though it would cost more. They hired a local carpenter who set up a woodworking shop right in the house to reproduce all of the wooden pieces and details and used a nearby mill to cut the wood.

Integrating Old and New

When it made sense (and saved her clients money) to use modern materials and methods, architect Facciolo didn't hesitate. For example,

above Remnants of the old kitchen have not been completely erased. An old plumbing chase in the outside wall was cleverly converted into a storage niche by adding shelves to display pottery.

she chose a laminate finish for the peninsula and adjacent countertop, instead of the soapstone used around the sink, to add contemporary style and functionality to that part of the kitchen.

For some details, the Beans had to find a stylistic middle ground. For example, they chose vintage-style Tiffany lamps to encourage a visual connection to the past and an old-fashioned soapstone sink, a typical 19th-century New England fixture that is popular once again. The same cannot be said about the appliances, however, which are all stainless steel. There is simply no way,

1 Pull-out
pantry drawers

ADDED INGREDIENTS

a soapstone tradition

■ One of the most authentic aspects of this old Vermont kitchen is the soapstone apron sink and adjoining countertops. Soapstone is soft, warm, natural, and traditional but resistant to

all sorts of food stains and acids. It is particularly apt since soapstone has been in use in kitchens in this part of the country for at least three centuries. The soapstone sink, which greatly predates the porcelain sink, was built locally from five plain slabs of stone glued together with a waterproof sealer. Undermounted on the soapstone countertop, it is a particularly old-time touch. Another traditional detail is the creation of drainage grooves machined into the countertop next to the sink, allowing the use of a dish rack without a pesky rubber pad underneath.

after all, to make a microwave oven, a six-burner pro-style gas cooktop, or a large, modern-day side-by-side refrigerator look Victorian, so the obvious choice was to embrace their modernity.

One aspect of the past that remains tied to the past is the oak door that guards the formal dining room. This heavy swinging door harks back to another time, yet like the new kitchen itself, it works beautifully in this age of flow, connection and classic eclecticism.

The new mudroom, a handy extra storage place behind the kitchen, is set behind a closable door so that it remains a separate transitional space between the kitchen and the outside.

1 In the redesigned pantry, shallow pull-out drawers were redesigned to accommodate staples.

2 The Beans installed a new generation of shelf carousels that rotate and swing out for easy access to storage in the corner cabinets.

3 The translucent pendant lamps, chosen for their retro style, produce a soft, gold-colored light.

4 The addition of an open display shelf over the refrigerator creates far more visual interest than plain cabinets would have.

2 Swivel corner storage rack

3 Pendant lights

4 Display shelf

"A throwback from the '60s that needed space"

Clever styling created a beauty on a budget

AFTER

An oversized window and modest budget dictated the scope of the remodel for this '60s-style kitchen, where knocking down walls and adding stepped-up cabinets and a surfboard-style breakfast bar updated its contemporary look.

WHEN THEY DECIDED TO REDO the kitchen of their 1963 California contemporary, Pat and Ron Eastman wanted it all. For starters, they needed an inexpensive makeover with few major structural changes. At the same time, they hoped for a brand-new kitchen with state-of-the-art appliances that retained the home's '60s spirit. Although there was no money in the budget for expansion, the renovated kitchen had to be airier, less cramped. The updated plan also had to include the existing large windows that defined the exterior of the house but add more storage and countertop work areas. Finally, they wanted to accomplish all of this without spending a lot of money.

Working with architect Peter Duxbury of Duxbury Architects in Los Altos, California, the Eastmans created a plan that allowed them to get exactly what they wanted. Duxbury used a handful of dramatic design touches to transform the space completely while keeping the scope of the renovation small.

BEFORE

The 40-year-old kitchen was showing signs of wear and tear, but it had good "bones," like this window.

Taking Stock

Pat Eastman knew from the start that she wanted to keep much about her original kitchen both for stylistic and budgetary reasons. And like many in her spot, she knew she faced some hard choices. She left the windows and much of the floor plan intact, and instead of adding cabinetry, she sacrificed a small hallway that led to the front door to use as a pantry. This far-more-useful food cupboard with open shelving also provided extra counter and drawer space. The change helped redefine the cluster of rooms around the kitchen, including the family room and a desk area, as a single, informal, and unified space. Overall, she was able to preserve much of the '60s style that first attracted her to the house.

Creating Focal Points

Cabinetry often plays a key role in renovating a kitchen. For the Eastmans, this was no different. The heart of the new design is a cluster of playfully staggered cabinets. These cabinets replace the wall that previously blocked off the kitchen from the next-door family room and contributed largely to the closed-off feel of the original space. This single device visually energizes the entire kitchen while it creates a partially open pass-through to the family room that adds dimension and light.

Positioned beneath the cabinets is a contemporary surfboard-style peninsula that is equipped with bar stools. Held in place by a simple round post and a matching table leg that was painted a pale turquoise, the peninsula has become not only a convenient gathering spot for informal dining or casual conversation but also serves as an interesting visual reference.

The rest of the kitchen shares the same minimal design as the peninsula. Light maple cabinets with flat full-overlay doors and slender pulls create a similar clean-lined, '60s-inspired look throughout the space. As a counterpoint to the wood cabinets, stainless steel is used for all of the appliances as well as for a backsplash behind the pro-style cooktop. To enhance the open and uncluttered look, the Eastmans decided to limit cabinet space, so they created a large walk-in pantry by closing off one end of a superfluous hallway next to the refrigerator. This efficient

facing page The cabinets make a visual bridge between the family room and kitchen. The new Corian peninsula, which previously had been concrete before it cracked, is a focal point.

before & after

The original kitchen was boxed in by walls, making the modest space feel even smaller. The simple kitchen renovation stayed within the existing footprint, which saved money.

BEFORE

Hallway

Kitchen

Dining room

Family room

AFTER

Pantry

Kitchen

Peninsula

Office

Family room

WHAT WE WANTED

walking on wood

■ Wooden floors are coming back to kitchens, replacing vinyl, linoleum, and tile. The reason is simple: Most kitchens remodeled these days are connected spatially and visually to the rooms surrounding them. To maintain the virtual flow of space, designers and homeowners choose continuous

flooring material. Still, although beautiful, wooden floors in the kitchen are not maintenance free. Although new hi-tech polyurethane finishes have made it possible for wooden floors to stand up better to the water, traffic, and abuse, they must be sealed with at least three coats of finish and refinished every few years for a hard-working space.

storage area is complete with shelving, drawers, and additional counter space.

Ultimately, the Eastmans got what they wanted: a light and airy kitchen that is both completely up to the minute and well suited to the original postwar-casual style of the house. The creative design opened up the kitchen, connecting it to the surrounding spaces, all with minimal reconstruction and expense—a successful study in creative wish fulfillment.

upclose

1 Unified design

2 Vintage details

Creative details, convenient storage, and unified design make this once-drab space really pop.

1 On the family-room side of the cabinet cluster, matching media cabinets carry the kitchen's style into the next room, creating an integrated look.

2 The vintage-design faucet was chosen to match the décor. The large picture windows left room for just a minimal backsplash.

3 Tucking a small drawer under the double wall ovens offers quick access to often-used pans.

4 The display shelf designed into this archway turns a passageway into a great spot to show off pottery.

3 Pot storage

4 Creative display

island romance

ISLANDS HAVE BECOME POPULAR in kitchen design, largely because they create a dramatic center point in any kitchen. Islands are also an elegant way to create a transition between work areas and the gathering and dining spaces. Also, since today's kitchens often need to accommodate more than one cook, the island has proven to offer a handy zone-separation device to keep multiple cooks from getting in each other's way. Keep in mind, though, that in addition to the size of the island itself, an island requires a minimum of 42 in. of open floor space on four sides. If your kitchen space is limited, a peninsula may be the better choice. A peninsula can deliver the advantages of an island in less space. A peninsula has only three open sides; thus it can accomplish many of the things an island can without gobbling up as much floor space.

Size

If an island or peninsula will be used for both cooking and dining, it needs to be large enough to have the seating, often bar stools, located a safe distance from any cooking surfaces. A good minimum width for multipurpose islands and peninsulas is 40 in., but wider is better.

Location

Islands and peninsulas not only add work space but also create boundaries. The location of an island or peninsula should be determined by the placement of the sink and the major appli-

above A small island makes sense in this modest-sized kitchen because it offers a convenient central work area that replaces the counter space lost to the large built-in refrigerator and wall oven along the back wall.

left This furniture-style island is stained a dark color to set it off from the white-painted cabinets around it. Open shelves on the living room side of the island are fitted with storage baskets that add charm and convenience, while the far side features cabinet doors for hidden storage.

left A well-designed peninsula can offer all of the features of an island while consuming less space. This one is fitted with a sink and three bar stools, making it an ideal perch for predinner refreshments.

ances as well as by traffic flow. If the island or peninsula is to be used primarily for food preparation, then it needs to be located near cooktops, ovens, and the refrigerator. Seating needs to be placed on the outer edge of the work area.

Style

Since an island or peninsula is often the focal point of a kitchen, style also needs to be considered. The island or peninsula should reflect that style in its use of cabinetry or shelving, its surfaces, and any hardware. Furniture-style islands are popular these days, and an island or peninsula should be chosen in much the way one would select any other piece of fine furniture, carefully considering form, function, and style.

above Even in this large kitchen, the owners opted to maximize their floor space by using a peninsula instead of an island. They fit it with a cooktop and surrounded it with bar stools, allowing the cook to converse with family and friends while preparing dinner.

"Country-cute in a ranch-style home"

A Prairie-Style renovation full of craft and detail

CREATING AN UTTERLY NEW KITCHEN that helps redefine the rest of the house is no small undertaking. For Rob and Joy Guttschow, it was essential. A few years ago, they bought an unadorned 1970s ranch-style house with an off-the-shelf kitchen in the Chicago suburbs. The Guttschows' master plan was to upgrade the house to match the spectacular ¾-acre lot it sat on and transform the house in stages into a charming Prairie-Style home.

Rob and Joy had fallen in love with the early 20th-century style, examples of which abound in the Midwest. Similar to the Stickley and Mission design styles, the Prairie Style was an offshoot of the Arts and Crafts movement and shares a devotion to natural materials, handcrafted workmanship, and spare abstract detailing. The Guttschows had researched the topic in depth and knew they had to start their plan with the most important room in their home, the kitchen. In pursuit of their new Prairie-Style kitchen, they hired Meyefski, Cook Architects of Glencoe, Illinois, whose principals also own Wickets Fine Cabinetry,

BEFORE

The old kitchen was a small, uninspired design that provided limited counter space.

AFTER

This expansive, furniture-style island with its rich green finish serves as both the visual and the functional center of this Prairie-Style kitchen. The island sink is 10 in. deep to make it easy to fill pots for the cooktop across from it.

before&after

A simple L-shaped design with space for a breakfast table was too dowdy for the renovation these homeowners had in mind. By eliminating the breakfast alcove and moving the interior wall back by 5 ft., the couple got the spacious kitchen with an island they had wanted.

BEFORE

Dining room

Kitchen

AFTER

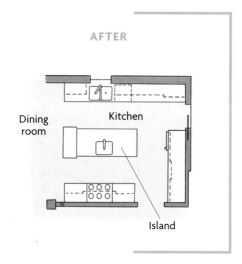

Dining room

Kitchen

Island

facing page The stylish armoire in the hall off of the kitchen disguises a pantry packed full of goods and gear.

a local shop with lots of experience designing Prairie-Style kitchens.

Working with partner Charles Cook, the Guttschows came up with a scheme for a new U-shaped kitchen organized around a central island, with cooking activities assigned primarily to one side of the kitchen and cleanup activities to the other. To make room for this new layout, the long interior wall of the space was moved back by 5 ft., while a former wall separating the kitchen from the dining room was removed completely.

Finding a Focal Point

To ensure that the kitchen reflected the strong Prairie Style the Guttschows were seeking, they knew they needed a strong focal point, and that turned out to be the center island. In keeping with the Prairie Style, the island is designed to be furniture-like rather than a simple built-in cabinet. It is made of rich green-stained cherry wood to enhance its stand-alone look. At one end of this island is a raised display cabinet that is several inches taller and a bit wider than the work surface behind it, so that the food preparation area is concealed from guests in the dining area that lies just beyond the kitchen. The island is fitted with several cabinets, drawers, and shelves, as well as a small but deep second sink and a tall, gooseneck faucet with a pull-out sprayer, a setup that is ideal for cleaning vegetables and for filling pots.

The new kitchen really comes alive, though, through the richness of its details. Among the most unusual of these are the wickets, or double doors, in the cabinets on either side of the cooktop, a specialty of Wickets Fine Cabinetry. Rob

Finding Your Style

ESSENTIAL STEP

Changing the style of this 1980s kitchen in a 1950s house to charming Prairie Style was the primary motivation to remodel. Elements of the style are found both in the layout and in the details the Guttschows and their architects designed into the kitchen. An essential ingredient is the ordered plan designed symmetrically around an island and open to the dining room. These now-common features were in those days a radical departure from compartmentalized Victorian architecture, and Frank Lloyd Wright was among the first to champion them. For example, the green accent tile, which matches the stain on the island, was a common element of Prairie-Style design.

in the furniture style

■ The novel and handsome armoire-style pantry cabinet that sits in the small hallway just outside the kitchen is the result of an artful cost-saving collaboration between the Guttschows and their architects. The couple knew from the time they began planning their project that they wanted some sort of pantry to store food staples and equipment without installing more cabinets in the kitchen proper that would add expense and take up valuable space. Initially they had intended to create a walk-in pantry closet, but as planning with Charles Cook moved forward, he convinced them that a more elegant solution would be to create a stand-alone furniture-style pantry cabinet. When the doors are closed, the armoire looks almost like a piece of fine furniture. Rob and Joy were directly involved in designing the interior layout with its combination of open shelves, swing-out shelves, and deep, bulk storage drawers to ensure that they got exactly the configuration they wanted.

and Joy were often directly involved in the design of these details, including the simple recess for a towel bar at one end of the island and the interior layout of the unique armoire-style pantry that sits in a hallway just outside the kitchen.

Even some of the seemingly ordinary choices in this kitchen were the result of careful thinking. The putty-colored, off-white paint on the outer cabinets, for example, was custom mixed by Wickets to match the traditional colors of the era. The plain white tiles in the backsplash behind the cooktop are turned 45 degrees to create a subtle but intriguing pattern. This diamond-shaped design is set off by a border of narrow green accent tiles that pick up on the green of the island. These minute details, hallmarks of the Prairie Style, combine to produce an inspired design.

above A set of handy drawers located under the pro-style gas cooktop makes food preparation convenient.

Stylish Yet Sensible

Despite its stylishly retro detailing, however, there is nothing old-fashioned about this kitchen. Up-to-date stainless-steel appliances, including a large cooktop, a wide refrigerator, and a double oven, make this a kitchen that is not only a pleasure to look at but also a joy to work in. The Guttschows managed to get everything they wanted—a kitchen that is utterly new yet perfectly reflects the warmth and charm of the Prairie Style they so dearly love.

ADDED INGREDIENTS

door within a door

■ One of the most innovative ideas in this kitchen is actually an old one. The architects designed a "wicket," or a small

door within a larger door, into each of the upper cabinets on either side of the cooktop. Behind each of these wicket doors is a shallow spice rack. When the wicket door is closed and the larger door is opened, the full cabinet is revealed. The inner and outer doors are hinged on opposite sides so that the larger door won't inadvertently open with

the smaller door. Wicket is a traditional English term for any door within a door, which was originally used to describe a

small access door within a castle or manor gate so people could pass in and out without opening the larger gate. In the 19th century, the idea migrated into the kitchen, resulting in a great way to maximize storage.

1 Recessed towel rack

the raised china cabinet at the end of the island serves to screen the working countertop area from the dining room, while creating a handy display storage space for tableware.

1 A simple recessed towel rack on the end of the island, an idea conceived by Joy that echoes the wicket style of the cabinets, is one of the many small details that add function and style.

2 A small tray cabinet with two tiers adds a tightly designed extra storage element to the island.

3 A shallow drawer under the cooktop keeps kitchen knives at the heart of the cooking area; deeper drawers hold pots and pans.

4 Not letting any space go to waste, the couple wanted this spice and condiment rack tucked up under the hood.

2 Tray
storage

3 Knife
drawer

4 Extra
spice rack

"A cramped kitchen that was cut off from the house"

A flexible entertaining space that spills into a backyard

AFTER

The new kitchen locates the principal cooking activities within a small footprint, allowing more area for dining and entertaining. The casual yet sophisticated breakfast bar visually separates the kitchen from the living area.

THE SIMPLE, MODERN KITCHEN that came with this bungalow when Norm Page and Jacqueline Bibeau bought it a few years ago had little to do with the charming style of the house or the way the couple saw themselves living in it. The fact is this couple had big dreams. Like most people, they wanted a new kitchen with a lot of function, but they couldn't spend a fortune to get it and had only the existing space of their first floor to work in. The couple longed for an indoor/outdoor space that would not only accommodate their love of cooking but also would let the kitchen communicate seamlessly with a new living/dining area and, even more importantly, with their large backyard, allowing them to entertain for business and for pleasure.

After bumping into each other for nearly a year in the original space, the couple was ready to make those dreams come true. In their plan, the first thing to go would be the extra bedroom and bath at the back of the house that blocked the kitchen from

BEFORE

The original kitchen was not only small and plain, but was too far from the backyard to satisfy the Bibeau's vision of a roomy, flexible space.

Defining Your Space

To get the little space they had to accomplish many things, Norm and Jacqueline intentionally left the boundaries within the kitchen, dining, and living space loosely defined. The only clear edge here is the breakfast bar that separates the kitchen's work area from the open space. This strategy allows each part of the room to borrow visual— and, if necessary, physical—space from all of the other parts. For example, the dining room, which sits at one end of the room, feels much larger because it shares visual space with the rest of the kitchen. Also, when it needs to be turned from dining space into a work area, that activity can easily expand into the adjoining space. None of these things would happen if the boundaries were too clearly defined.

the warm California sunshine just outside. Getting rid of these would create more room and make possible a wall of glass doors that would open onto a spacious new patio.

Into this open space, they wanted to put a kitchen that could easily shift gears from quiet haven to work area to party mode, intimate enough for the two of them to enjoy when they were alone but big enough to handle a crowd. Since Jacqueline, who is a partner in a small ad agency, works at home, she also needed the kitchen to work occasionally as a businesslike gathering space for meetings that might overflow from her upstairs office.

They worked up a plan to turn the back half of their first floor into a friendly, multitasking space with San Francisco architect Michael Mullin. By simply demolishing a few walls, Mullin's design created a spare, open space with intimate charm and wide-open energy and did it within the couple's tight budget. Although the demolition required Norm and Jacqueline to move out of the house for three months, the results proved worthwhile. The new kitchen/dining area includes a large, open space spanning the back of the house with room for a small reading corner and designated dining area, all of which spill into the backyard through three wide pairs of glass doors.

A Hardworking Kitchen

The working heart of the kitchen is a well-laid-out, well-equipped space with lots of gear, counters, and storage designed into a surprisingly small footprint. The kitchen has lots of clever storage ideas squeezed cleanly into out-of-the-way places, such as the small pantry closet that just fits under

above The wide glass doors swing out to transform the kitchen and dining alcove into an open, welcoming, indoor/outdoor space, perfect for parties and enjoying the California sun.

left Although the working part of the kitchen is relatively small, it now benefits from the increased space and sun exposure in the dining area.

indoor outdoor floors

■ Slate tile was used for the floor here for a variety of stylistic and functional reasons. First, it is weather resistant enough to use outside as well as in, allowing Mullin to create a continuous

floor surface that covers the kitchen and dining area then moves outside onto the patio, with no interruption but a piece of weather stripping. Second, in this kitchen the slate picks up the black horizontal lines of the soapstone counters. Finally, it is an ideal transmitter of the radiant floor heating used here. But slate is a popular choice in any kitchen because its soft and porous texture feels warm and comfortable underfoot. This texture, though, means that it needs to be sealed on installation and resealed every year or so.

the stairs. It's also loaded with hardworking equipment such as the six-burner, pro-style cooktop, double wall ovens, a beefy refrigerator, a farm-style sink, and a professional-grade electric mixer. Typical of the thoughtful organization at work here, the mixer sits on a swing-up shelf that can be pulled out quickly or stowed invisibly back in its cabinet. In fact, all of this well-designed efficiency frees up the open spaces of the room to be simply, well, open.

The clean, custom maple cabinets are done in a spare Shaker style. Soapstone countertops and slate tile floors provide a warm, traditional nuance, while they create a contemporary-looking horizontal expanse of black stone to offset the light cabinets. Such vintage touches as an apron-front farm-style sink are accompanied by just enough stainless steel in the form of appliances, the vent hood, and the backsplash to keep the look up to date.

before & after

In the old plan, the prime real estate on the first floor was occupied by a bedroom and bath that the couple was happy to trade for a bigger and better kitchen. The remodeled plan includes the wall of glass doors the couple desired while delivering enough space to handle activities from breakfast to work to entertaining.

BEFORE

Bedroom

Bedroom

Dining room

Kitchen

AFTER

Bedroom

Dining room

Kitchen

Glass block

left The kitchen was designed with a six-burner cooktop and a pair of wall ovens close together with counter space in between to keep the cooking activity all within one area.

below The wall of glass bricks above the counters lets in sunshine but maintains the couple's privacy.

An Elegant Alcove

A breakfast bar separates the kitchen from the open space that includes an ample area for mingling, a small but elegant dining alcove, and even a place to sit and read. It also includes a counter fitted with additional upper and lower cabinets for storage, which, in effect, serves as an extension of the kitchen itself. The counter also has a small sink and two wine chillers—one for white and one for red—so that it easily turns into a bar when the occasion arises. The dining alcove at the

far end of the open area is furnished with an intimate dining table and eight upholstered chairs.

Along the back of the house, the glass doors open onto a terrace that is built to the same level as the kitchen floor and uses the same slate tiles, so that on warm evenings, of which there many in this part of the world, the life of the kitchen flows easily in and out without interruption.

above To add storage to the new kitchen, this shallow pantry closet was created along a wall of the back hall, making good use of otherwise wasted space.

upclose

1 Pantry closet

althrough no larger than the old kitchen, the working space of the new kitchen is filled with features that pump up its usability.

1 In the recess under the stairway, Mullin carved out a pair of storage cabinets with shelves that pull out for easy access.

2 Pull-out drawer shelves make the small storage cabinet beneath the microwave easy to use.

3 The stainless-steel backsplash between the cooktop and vent hood features integrated shelves to keep spices and utensils handy.

4 Beneath the cooktop, two large pot drawers offer easy storage for bulky cooking equipment.

2 Pull-out shelves

3 Integrated shelves

4 Oversized pot drawers

storage strategies

mAKING THE MOST OF YOUR EXISTING storage options while coming up with creative new ones may ultimately keep your remodeling costs down by minimizing the amount of cabinetry you will have to buy. It will also increase your enjoyment of your finished kitchen by making everything easy to find.

Base Cabinets

Easy ways to maximize the storage you have available in your base cabinets include:

PULL-OUT SHELVES. Base cabinets with doors and open shelves are the least expensive configuration. By adding pull-out shelves on rollers, you will make the items stored at the back easier to get to.

DRAWERS. Drawers are the most efficient way to store equipment that you want to reach in a hurry but are more expensive than cabinets with doors. Use deep storage drawers for big pots and pans or other bulky items.

CORNER STORAGE. To ensure that the deep corner spaces where base cabinets meet don't turn into dead space, add a lazy Susan-style carousel or one of the new high-tech, double-tiered, wire rack systems.

APPLIANCE SHELVES. A lift-up shelf that pops in and out of a base cabinet is a great way to store a heavy appliance, such as an electric mixer or food processor.

Pantries

A good-sized and well-situated pantry can provide an easy and inexpensive way to store lots of canned and dry food plus extra cooking gear that would other-

above Finding creative ways to make new storage options is a great way to keep costs down. Using the dead space within this bench for storage is like getting a free extra cabinet.

right Pop-up storage shelves save precious counter space by making it easy to store often-used appliances out of the way yet easy to retrieve.

wise require expensive cabinets. You don't need a big, old-fashioned butler's pantry; instead, consider putting shelves in an old broom closet or infrequently used coat closet, install shelving under a stairway or in an odd nook, or close off an inconvenient passageway.

Display Storage

Open shelving on a wall, in an island, or under a counter is an attractive and inexpensive way to store things you want to show off, such as fine china, glassware, or cookbooks.

Deep Storage

Create storage spaces for infrequently used items wherever you can by using benches (add a hinged lid) and out-of-the-way shelves (like above the refrigerator) to keep things you don't need often.

above Open shelves with pretty objects you want to show off, like pottery or glassware, or with attractive baskets are a great way to save a little money on cabinet construction while adding charm.

above Large-capacity deep drawers are essential for bulky objects like cooking pots or metal bowls but are not recommended for breakable ware.

"A kitchen so small that the fridge sat in the hallway"

THE SOLUTION

An eco-friendly kitchen with Depression-era roots

WHEN ERICA SMITH AND JIM RIGGS bought their bungalow in the Oakland Hills of California, they inherited a too-small kitchen that had barely been touched since the house was built in the 1930s. Narrow swinging doors at either end of the worn-out kitchen led to a dark hallway with a stairwell at one end and a cramped eating area at the other. Space in the kitchen itself was so limited that the refrigerator was stuck in the hallway by the stairs. Because the windows and the adjoining areas were very small, the entire kitchen end of the house was cast in a dark pall. In short, they needed to eliminate the walls between the kitchen and the adjoining spaces, get creative with their work space, and bring in some more light.

As is often the case in old city neighborhoods, especially around San Francisco, the lot their house sat on was tiny and had no yard to speak of, so any outward expansion was impossible. The couple also had neither the budget nor the appetite for taking on a large renovation project, inside or out. Whatever they did

AFTER

Fewer walls, bigger windows, and the use of open shelves add to the sense of space in this modest-sized kitchen. Beautifully hand-crafted cabinets mixed with green materials also make this kitchen unique.

BEFORE

Decades of paint buildup and cracking plaster had caught up with the once charming kitchen the couple started with, while a chopped-up layout made it hard for them to use.

above The new design, which includes beautiful casement windows, connects the dining nook visually with the kitchen, eliminating the cramped feeling of the old space without building any square footage.

right Low-volatility varnish was used to finish the cabinets, reducing the amount of chemicals introduced into the air. New materials such as cork floors and quartz composite countertops minimize the environmental impact and give the kitchen a fresh look.

had to happen within the existing footprint of the kitchen and the two small rooms at either end of it. Also, they wanted to replace the hand-built (and now badly worn out) Depression-era kitchen with one that evoked much of the simple craftsmanship of the period. But more, the couple, both graphic designers and keen on innovation, also wanted to try out new—especially natural—environmentally friendly materials wherever possible.

To redesign their kitchen, they turned to architect Henry Siegel of Siegel and Strain Architects, an award-winning firm in nearby Emeryville, California, that has a special interest in both historic and environmentally sustainable design. Siegel began by removing the wall between the kitchen and the stair hall and replacing it with a small half-wall. Now a new refrigerator could take its proper place in the kitchen. At the other end of the kitchen, he widened the narrow doorway between the kitchen and the breakfast nook, creating an archway framed by two pedestal-like half-walls that echoed the other half-wall. Finally, he designed larger windows for all three spaces to allow fresh sunshine to flood the kitchen area.

Sustainable Style

Wherever possible, Siegel specified the use of "green" products, materials that have the least impact on the environment. Being green in the context of a kitchen-remodeling project in an old house in an urban neighborhood is, of course, a relative thing. Erica and Jim focused on using products that made sense for their design goals and budget—cork floor, engineered stone or quartz composite counters, energy-efficient appliances, low-volatility finishes that give off minimal

Defining Your Space

ESSENTIAL STEP

Given the limitations of their house and lot, Erica and Jim accomplished a lot within an established footprint that could not change. By removing walls at either end of their old kitchen, they were able to create a long, open room that instantly transformed wasted space. At the center is the working heart of the kitchen, designed around a long, shallow U-shaped counter. In the middle of the U, a stainless-steel sink is located beneath two large windows. At either end of the U are two under-the-counter shelves that serve as bookcases, which open into the passages that lead into and out of the main kitchen. (On the kitchen side, these bookshelves are cleverly disguised with faux-cabinet doors.) On the interior wall, two glass-fronted cabinets bracket a professional-style range with a simple stainless vent hood. To squeeze still more out of their layout, the homeowners opted for slightly bigger cabinets than the originals and packed them with efficient storage solutions.

cabinetry tricks

■ By having their cabinets built by their contractor (who is also a cabinetmaker), Erica and Jim were able to fine-tune the storage space exactly to fit their needs and specifications without adding significantly to the cost of the new kitchen. For example,

they opted for oversized drawers under the counters in place of typical door-fronted cabinets. Small, shallow drawers are nested within the top drawers to store knives, pot holders, and towels. Other nifty details that boost the storage quotient include two-stage, swing-out storage racks used in the corners of the base cabinets and sized-to-fit, slide-out cabinets on either side of the range, one for spices and one for trays.

above The key shape of the newly widened arch lets light through at the top, while the indentations at the bottom accommodate base cabinets and counters on the kitchen side.

facing page By getting rid of the wall separating the kitchen from the stair hall, the design benefits from the light that the single-pane stairway windows bring into the space.

hazardous fumes, and maple wood from sustainable forests—but did not stretch the point.

Other facets of the kitchen are simple yet beautifully designed. In the kitchen itself, Erica chose custom, naturally finished maple cabinets and made sure they were configured exactly as she'd envisioned. For example, she wanted over-sized drawers below the counter and open display shelves above, among other features. This sort of custom detail would have been difficult, if not impossible, to find in factory-built cabinets.

The couple chose stainless-steel appliances to offset the pale mellowness of the light maple and

to add a contemporary touch. Modern white handcrafted tiles along the backsplash and cream-colored quartz composite counters add a sense of crispness to the kitchen, while keeping the look light and bright.

Arty Alcoves

Between the kitchen and the dining alcove, the old archway was raised and widened to allow more sunlight into the kitchen. Within the alcove, a set of built-in benches in the style of the cabinets was added to anchor the dining nook and to provide storage. The pale yellow walls were hand-rubbed with coffee-dipped rags to age the paint and add an artisanal feeling to the space. This was also an environmentally friendly alternative to applying a heavy chemical treatment. A swinging door leading from the alcove to the adjoining dining room was replaced with a far

A wall at one end of the kitchen reduced the usable space and cut off access to the refrigerator, while a small doorway to the eating nook blocked sunshine. By knocking down a wall and widening a doorway, the couple gained space and light for their new kitchen.

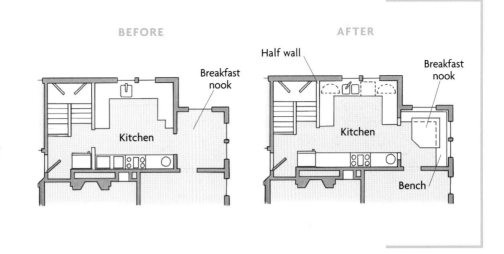

BEFORE

Breakfast nook

Kitchen

AFTER

Half wall

Breakfast nook

Kitchen

Bench

putting cork on it

■ Erica and Jim chose cork flooring because it has the same warm look and give underfoot as linoleum and vinyl; it's durable, resilient, and natural looking; and it adds sound and heat insulation to any floor installation. Cork is especially pop-

ular with green, or sustainable, designers because it naturally resists moisture and mold without resorting to any chemical additives. It is hypoallergenic and produces no outgassing, which means that it won't give off any of the unpleasant or unsafe fumes that are common with chemically treated flooring. The cork flooring

in this kitchen is made of interlocking 3-ft. by 1-ft. planks of engineered wood with a cork veneer, but cork also is available as tiles.

more practical sliding pocket door. Two huge French-style windows open at the back of the alcove behind the bench.

Over the dining table, which is fitted with a space-efficient, sturdy restaurant base, a hand-blown Italian glass pendant lamp mixes old-school craft with fresh fancifulness. A similar pendant lamp graces the hallway and stairwell that were once so dark. It's the perfect finishing touch for this delightfully integrated, well-executed kitchen.

upclose

1 Tray storage

to keep the kitchen light, spacious, and efficient, it is filled with inventive storage and design ideas.

1 Rather than waste the narrow space above the refrigerator, the homeowner designed this cabinet in which to keep wide, flat items such as trays, platters, and baking sheets.

2 A custom-designed storage drawer beside the stove keeps spices and other condiments handy.

3 With high-tech stainless steel above and below, the handcrafted tiles of the backsplash add a warmer, textured touch.

4 Convenient shallow drawers to store pot lids and utensils are nested into several of the drawers around the kitchen.

2 Pull-out storage

3 Tile backsplash

4 Slide-out spice drawer

"An '80s nightmare in black and white"

Mid-Century chic in this '50s-era home

ONCE THEIR THREE CHILDREN reached school age, these homeowners knew they needed a bigger, more smartly organized kitchen. The small kitchen of their Dallas home, the product of a 20-year-old remodeling project done before they bought the house, was inadequate for their growing needs. And it had little to do with the original style of their vintage 1950s ranch, a style that they particularly loved.

They wanted a kitchen that would serve as "command central" for their busy family life, with an open, free-flowing floor plan that allowed the kitchen to borrow space from a nearby family room. They also yearned for a kitchen that recalled the space-age style of the late 1950s and early 1960s, a style known as Mid-Century Modern. In addition to living in their dream house, they had for years been collecting pottery and other design objects from the era by such designers as Russell Wright. It was this sort of spare aesthetic that the homeowners wanted echoed in the surfaces and details in the new kitchen.

AFTER

Unadorned cabinets, stainless-steel appliances, and a judicious choice of ultramodern furniture and fixtures give this kitchen a youthful Mid-Century Modern style.

BEFORE

A little laminate can be a good thing, but in this old kitchen it was practically the only thing.

Finding Your Style

The spare look of this kitchen grew out of the home-owners' commitment to recapturing the feeling of the original 1955 style of the house and evoking the Mid-Century Modern design of the 1950s and 1960s arts and crafts objects that they collect. At the same time, they wanted their kitchen to be practical. Designer David Cadwallader, a noted practitioner of the postwar contemporary style, chose the unadorned maple cabinets, the dining table, and the pale-green glass backsplash that define the clean-lined look of the room. He also picked the light maple flooring and the chairs that recall the Mid-Century Modern style as well. Iconic period pieces such as a sunburst wall clock and space-age-style pendant lamps over the island and dining table unify the design.

quickfixes

Infusing the kitchen with personal interests or passions—be they in the form of Colonial tools, English bone china, or, in this owner's case, 1950s American pottery—is a great way to put your stamp on a new kitchen.

above The open shelving the architects placed between the kitchen and the family room creates a boundary between the two spaces while keeping a visually open connection. It also provides an ideal place to display pottery.

Making Modern Lines

To come up with a remodeling plan that would provide the structural backdrop for the décor they envisioned, they turned to Bruce Bernbaum and Patricia Magadini of Bernbaum-Magadini Architects in Dallas. As the lynchpin of this whole-house renovation, the kitchen was moved to a more central location and joined to an informal dining area and a new family room. The architects also removed walls and replaced them with open shelving that let the spaces flow visually into one another.

The structural design is essentially an idealized version of the original 1950s look of the house. The new kitchen is designed in a simple U shape with a built-in refrigerator anchoring the left leg of the U and a double-door pantry cabinet anchoring the right. The contemporary cabinets are made of light-colored maple, fitted with flat

above The central island serves as a food preparation station, family breakfast bar, and, especially with its small bar sink, as a casual entertainment center.

doors and drawers and minimalist hardware and cabinet pulls that are all but invisible. On either side of the U, the wall cabinets are double stacked, with a second set of upper cabinets rising all the way to the 11-ft. ceiling, which enhances the modern lines of the kitchen while creating some bonus storage space.

In the center of the U is a large 6-ft. by 4-ft. island with a breakfast bar and three stools for

a splash of glass

■ The green glass backsplash is one of the most eye-catching features of this kitchen's design. This relatively simple detail offers an easy way of creating an elegant and low-maintenance surface behind the countertop for about the cost of tile. Backed with a light-colored paint and attached with silicone

adhesive, this glass element makes the counters look more sparkly. A glass back-splash is typically fabri-cated in 3-ft. to 6-ft. panels by a glass or mirror shop, which coats the back with silicone-based "opaci" paint that expands and contracts.

Frosted glass is often used to diffuse the color, minimize the presence of the paint, and cut down on glare. Variations on this design include using ribbed, fluted, etched, or sand-blasted glass.

quick meals. The island is fitted with a small second sink for food preparation and occasional duty as a bar sink. The kitchen is designed with oversize 54-in. spaces between the island and the counters, far wider than the standard 42 in., a feature intended to amplify the openness of the kitchen as well as accommodate an active family life and loads of guests.

Integrating the '50s Sensibility

Above the long counter on the sink wall is a set of high, narrow windows designed intentionally to shield the interior from the blazing Texas sun. On either side of the windows are open shelves that display part of their vintage 1950s pottery collection. Below these shelves is a continuous back-splash of green frosted glass, which complements the kitchen's pale-green granite countertops.

The backsplash, which helps to define this kitchen's paradoxical up-to-the-minute yet retro style, was the creation of David Cadwallader, a local designer who is nationally recognized for integrating 1950s style into 21st-century décor. He was brought into the project to flesh out the

before&after

The original kitchen, little more than an extension of a hallway, had limited counter space, little storage area, and not enough room for a young family. The architects situated the new kitchen at the center of the house, connecting it spatially to the dining area and family room, newly fashioned at the back of the house.

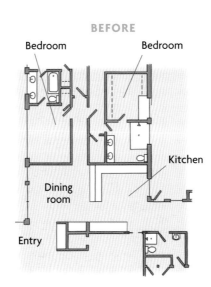

BEFORE

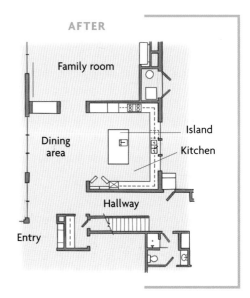

AFTER

left The island was designed with enough width to ensure that kids dining at the breakfast bar would be out of the way of the food preparation. Pendant lights provide useful task lighting for cooking and for eating casual meals but can be dimmed for entertaining.

above The high cabinets that reach all the way to the ceiling contribute to the trim, uncluttered look of the kitchen and serve as a structural backdrop for the room's retro styling.

decorative design of the kitchen, adding such pop elements as the sunburst wall clock and the egg-shaped pendant lamps above the island.

Beyond the island is an informal dining area with a contemporary table also designed by Cadwallader and a set of contemporary plywood chairs chosen by him to capture the spirit of Mid-Century Modern spirit without slavishly imitating it. Likewise, the translucent pendant lamp above the table and the bar stools at the island, both of which are recent designs selected by Cadwallader, evoke 1950s minimalism but are totally contemporary.

Tying It Together

Pale maple floors throughout the space tie together the sprawling open plan of the kitchen and the adjoining rooms. In the opening between the

COOK'S CORNER

the second sink

■ Putting a second sink in the island added lots of extra functionality to this kitchen without costing much money. Although the main sink is located not too far away, this one allows more than one person to work in the kitchen at the same time. Both are fitted with disposals, tall, arched faucets, and pull-out sprayers so most tasks can be performed at either sink (although because the main sink is closer to the dishwasher, it's much more convenient for cleanup). When the couple is entertaining, the island does double duty as a buffet, with the sink serving either as a bar sink or as an ice bucket to keep a couple of bottles of wine chilling.

1 Display shelves

dining area and the family room, a low cabinet partition with open shelves above it is used to display more of the pottery collection.

With wide-open spaces within and around the kitchen and ready access to lots of storage space and state-of-the-art cooking equipment, this kitchen indeed is "command central" for this active household. But it is also a marvelous work of modern art.

t he clean look of the kitchen may be inspired by the past, but its features are all about present-day function.

1 Open shelves between the kitchen and family room were designed to display pottery and provide a semi-open partition.

2 Shelves on rollers make retrieving heavy items a simpler task.

3 Deep drawers provide handy storage for bulky items.

4 A clean, solid wall of flat cabinetry hides two sets of upper cabinets and a spacious oversize pantry closet.

2 Roll-out cabinet shelves

3 Deep storage drawers

4 Wall of flat cabinetry

"A kitchen that was smaller than the laundry room"

THE SOLUTION

A warm, open cook's kitchen with plenty of room for fun

AFTER

This pleasant country kitchen mixes casual comfort with lots of function. A baking center is playfully tucked into the curve of an existing wall, while the two-tone island adds to the kitchen's eclectic style.

SOMETIMES A NEW HOME APPEARS to have everything—location, price, size, and views—but is encumbered by a kitchen that is too small, out of date, badly laid out, dark, or all of the above. This was the situation this young couple faced when they bought their 1971 country contemporary in northern Vermont a few years ago. The views and light convinced them to buy it anyway, despite the kitchen that came with it, which they decided would have to be completely remodeled.

After living with the old kitchen for nearly two years, they formed a wish list that included not just something bigger but a space that could grow with their two small children, comfortably handle their big family holiday dinners (often cooked by the husband), and accommodate the wife's avid baking activities. Still, they weren't sure how to create a larger kitchen or how to arrange for all of the details they wanted, like an island, a baking station for her, more storage and elbow room, modern appliances, a dining table—and even an antique rocking chair.

BEFORE

Two was a crowd in the old kitchen, which was a big problem for this pair of dedicated chefs.

Taking Stock

In this house, the original floor plan was poorly designed with cabinets blocking the best outdoor views and light and with a laundry room that was larger than the kitchen. The owners knew they'd have to renovate but weren't sure how big a project that was going to be. After living with the old kitchen for nearly two years, they decided that they would have to totally reorganize the way space was used and move around some windows and doors in exterior walls. Resolving this issue then helped them understand the scope, relative cost, and emotional commitment that they were looking at (more than a simple upgrade but slightly less than a total renovation). It also helped them understand that they needed to hire an architect rather than leave structural changes to a contractor. For example, they would never have thought to add this surprise cutout window on their own, which breaks up the wall space and brings a framed view of the trees into the room.

Working with an Architect

One thing was obvious: Walls would have to come down or be moved—and that included possibly rearranging windows and doors in the exterior wall. Given that fact, it was clear to the owners that they needed an architect, and they hooked up with Irene Facciolo of Thunder Mill Design in Montpelier, Vermont. Together, the couple and Facciolo decided on a floor plan that moved the kitchen into a space originally occupied by an oversized laundry room. This not only allowed them to have more kitchen space but also opened up the sunny southern wall previously blocked by kitchen cabinets and turned that space into a lively dining and gathering area.

Within this floor plan, Facciolo created a kitchen that is simple, warm, and efficient. Along the back wall is a long countertop that includes a farmer-style sink made of Vermont soapstone and a gas cooktop with a stainless vent hood. Above

above An open plate rack over the sink allows for the quick storage and retrieval of dishes and adds to the farmhouse feel of the kitchen.

above The built-in cabinetry has the feeling of old-fashioned kitchen "furniture," which was common in New England kitchens a century ago. Along with the crown molding, stained to match the island, the cabinetry highlights the kitchen's country charm.

baking central

Both members of this couple are enthusiastic cooks, but she has a special interest in baking. To handle the two of them working in the kitchen at the same time, the architect created a center at

one end of the room where the wife keeps all of her baking supplies. It is partly enclosed by a curved wall that was part of the laundry room. The butcher block countertop is large enough to give her adequate work and storage space. The countertop is also set at a height of 32 in., 4 in. shorter than the other counters in the kitchen in order to give her the leverage she requires to work dough. A slotted storage area under the counter holds her baking sheets, and the double-door cabinet stows pans and bowls. Opposite the baking center on the island rests a piece of soapstone that she can use to roll out dough, and then pop it in the oven positioned just below.

the counter are an open dish rack, a wrought-iron pot rack, and a clever built-in spice rack. Under the counter, useful drawers for holding cookware are tucked in next to the dishwasher.

Most of the major storage functions are consigned to a designated pantry area to the right of the long counter. Large, custom-built cabinets and a built-in refrigerator stand on either side of a small counter topped by still more cabinets and a microwave. At the opposite end of the long counter is another custom-built cupboard designed as a dedicated place to house the wife's baking and bread-making supplies. All of the cabinetry is made of durable, light-colored maple that is lightly finished to give the kitchen a casual, rustic look.

Cooking on an Island

At the center of the kitchen is a friendly yet hardworking island. The oven is placed at the baking end of the island for the wife's convenience. A small second sink is positioned at the opposite end of the island so that the couple can work easily in the kitchen at the same time. For practicality, the island is topped with butcher block (as

before & after

A laundry room consumed most of the floor area and left the old kitchen squeezed up against the back wall. The new kitchen is designed to face the light and incorporates a nearby eating and gathering area.

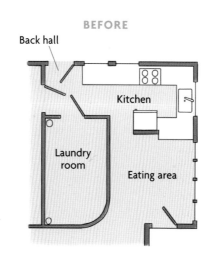

BEFORE

Back hall

Kitchen

Laundry room

Eating area

AFTER

Pantry

Kitchen

Eating area

Baking center

left To maintain tightly controlled work zones in the new kitchen, the soapstone sink and drain board, overhead dish rack, and dishwasher are clustered together in one small corner.

below To put the oven right where the homeowner needed it, Facciolo took the unusual step of placing it in the island right below the soapstone rolling board in the butcher-block top and handy to the baking center.

is the baking center), while the island's base is stained a traditional brick red. A piece of soapstone has been inserted into the butcher block at the baking end of the island to use as a pastry board. (The section of the countertop cut out to accommodate the sink was used to create the soapstone insert.) On one side of the island, the butcher-block top overhangs by 1 ft. to create space for a pair of stools that provide perches for guests, kids, or off-duty cooks.

Heavenly Hangout

Beyond the island is a dining area with a farmer's table, plus two rocking chairs for the couple and their two small children to watch the sunset after

ADDED INGREDIENTS

local color

■ This couple chose native Vermont soapstone for their counter-tops early in the process, but they also wanted a traditional farm-style apron-front soapstone sink with a grooved drain board milled into the counter surface. For the same reasons why people enjoy soapstone counters—the soft, warm feel of the stone—many also find it attractive for sinks, as they have for centuries. Long used as a sink material, soapstone brings authenticity to a vintage-style country kitchen, but it can become chipped more easily than other materials. However, for the homeowner, the nicks that now adorn her soapstone sink have just added to its charm.

1 Tray storage

the new kitchen uses several smart storage and design features in the island and cabinets to pack a lot into a limited space.

1 Tray storage racks in the baking center keep cookie sheets and pastry boards close to the action.

2 One great advantage of having a cooktop separate from the oven is that the space below can be used for pot storage.

3 The soapstone insert added to the butcher block is ideal for preparing food.

4 The second sink, fitted with a hot-water dispenser for making tea or instant soup, leaves the main sink free for another cook.

a well-prepared meal. The space, which is nicely separated from the cooking area by the island, doubles as the central play area. When the kid stuff is cleared away and friends (and their kids) come over for dinner, the party never leaves the room. The new kitchen is all they had hoped for—not only bigger and more workable but also a warm, comfortable place where, as the wife says, "you just want to hang out."

2 Pot storage

3 Soapstone insert

4 Second sink

above To make your refrigerator disappear into the cabinetry and take on the look of a traditional built-in icebox, you can easily add cabinet-style panels.

left Dishwashers with two drawers that can be operated separately offer a way for one or two people to run small loads as needed.

appliance science

THE APPLIANCES YOU CHOOSE for your kitchen greatly influence its function, layout, and style. Appearance can be easily modified with cabinet panels that create a built-in look. Most special features are available across brands, so choose appliances that suit your culinary needs and fit appropriately in your kitchen.

Refrigerators

Refrigerators come in several formats.

Side-by-Side. The doors require less space to open and create less traffic disruption. The resulting narrow compartments make it tough to store wide platters.

Bottom-Mounted Freezer. A pull-out freezer situated below the refrigerator puts the main compartment at convenient eye level. The door swing on a 36-in. unit is large.

Top-Mounted Freezer. You bend over to retrieve food from the refrigerator section.

Refrigerator Drawers. Space in a main refrigerator is saved by storing some items in refrigerator drawers, installed under a counter or in an island.

Stoves, Cooktops, and Microwave Ovens

A stove with a cooktop and an oven in a single unit is a good choice for kitchens where space is tight; it is also cost effective. A cooktop with a separate wall oven (or two) lets you create storage below the cooktop and puts the oven at eye level for easy viewing and access, but this requires more space and costs

above A pair of refrigerator drawers, also available as freezer drawers, lets you put produce or drinks right where you want them under the counter and gives you a way of downsizing your refrigerator.

above Having the refrigerator and freezer situated side-by-side is the most popular style because it creates the smallest door swing, but it also produces tall, narrow interiors not suited to wide containers.

left A popular feature is the through-the-door ice and water dispenser that lets you retrieve these necessary items without constantly opening the refrigerator door.

more. Microwave ovens are a staple these days, and most homeowners welcome having them built-in.

Dishwashers

Most manufacturers offer a wide range of useful features like stainless-steel interiors, adjustable shelves, and energy-saver settings. A new generation of two-drawer dishwashers makes it easier to do small loads of dishes; these are currently available from only one company, Fisher & Paykel®. Generally, the more features you choose, the more you will pay.

left By having the cooktop installed separately from the oven, you make it easier for two people to cook at the same time and leave the space below the cooktop for useful storage.

"The first renovation just didn't work"

A multipurpose space that's great for hanging out

tHE ORIGINAL KITCHEN IN THIS DOWNTOWN Philadelphia residence was the result of the makeover the owners did when they bought the top-floor apartment 18 years ago. "The kitchen was the one mistake we made," they admit. "It was too small, and we ended up with a series of chopped-up spaces." Working with architect Neil Sandvold, who had helped them with their previous renovation, the couple was committed to getting it right.

This time the plan was simple: Combine several functions in one shared space instead of walling them off into separate rooms. By reworking what they had, the owners were able to create an open kitchen and family room with much more usable space. The effect of combining the rooms has transformed the way they live in their kitchen area, especially now that their children are grown. They find themselves spending much more time just being together in the newly expanded kitchen.

One big benefit of the expanded kitchen is that the couple can now share the space while cooking,

AFTER

A tightly organized cooking area anchors the beautiful new space that resulted from the renovation. Room for the work island, which doubles as a gathering spot, is one bonus of the open plan.

BEFORE

The pot rack from the old kitchen, seen here during construction, was kept in place while everything but the stove was demolished.

Defining Your Space

When this couple redesigned their apartment, they knocked down the walls between four small rooms: the original kitchen, a den, a sauna, and a storage closet. In addition, by eliminating a wall of closets in the old kitchen, space for a larger island was created. This island, together with the more efficiently organized cabinet system, actually created much more storage space. The former den became the sitting area of the new kitchen, while the sauna and storage closet became the new den that is also open to the kitchen space. By sharing a single space, these three functional areas—the kitchen, the kitchen sitting area, and the den—remain close enough for easy conversation. They are spacious enough to handle a crowd of friends yet provide privacy when needed.

quickfixes

A traditional hanging pot rack works beautifully—it's convenient and the shiny cluster is an interesting counterpoint to the clean, uncluttered design of the cabinetry.

eating, reading, working, or even just watching television, something they previously did in separate rooms.

Forming Function

At the center of the new design is a large granite-topped work island that doubles as a breakfast bar with room for three stools—the perfect place for morning coffee or light dining. Wrapped around the island is an L-shaped kitchen area with a 36-in. pro-style range, a sink, a dishwasher, and additional counter space, all backed by a stainless-steel backsplash. Beyond the island, the activity flows immediately to a nearby desk made of matching cabinetry. Thanks to a small wine rack integrated into the desk, it also doubles as a serving area when guests come over. A sofa and chair focused on a 42-in. flat-screen television converts what used to be a detached den into a cozy family sitting area. To one side of this is a round breakfast table that the couple also uses as a casual dinner table. Another semiseparate but connected sitting area is just beyond the television screen and has sweeping views of the city.

Modular Work

The result is a room large enough to contain a variety of simultaneous functions, yet one that still works as a single, intimate space where every part feels connected to the rest. One reason for this sense of unity is the versatile European cabinet system the couple installed in their new kitchen. Its modular design allowed them to use it throughout the space in various configurations for the kitchen cabinets as well as for the desk, the pantry cupboard, the bookshelves, and an enclosure for the refrigerator. The effect is to strengthen the visual connection from one part of the space to another.

left With three stools tucked under, the island is easily converted to a conversation bar for guests.

below Although everything else is new, the couple saw no reason not to keep the range and the pot rack that had been essential parts of their old kitchen.

before & after

The old plan featured a claustrophobic collection of small rooms, the sizes of which limited the use of each. By combining the space of two rooms, the new plan allows each area to borrow from the other and create a greater whole.

BEFORE

Island

Den

Kitchen

Whirlpool

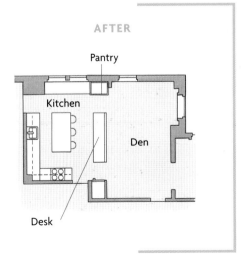

AFTER

Pantry

Kitchen

Den

Desk

imported ingenuity

■ At the heart of this design is the German-made cabinet system that gives the kitchen an efficient, contemporary look. The system comes with a huge selection of design and storage options, increasing its flexibility and functionality and allowing

the couple to pick exactly the features they needed. Also, since they chose a less costly laminate finish, the price was comparable to what they might have paid for a good domestic-built cabinet system.

The central work island doubles as a breakfast bar and hides handy refrigerator drawers. A pantry cabinet has roll-out storage and drawers for food staples, utensils, and linens. The refrigerator is built into an identical cabinet. The system allows many cabinets and appliances to disappear into a cohesive style with the overall effect of a unified, clutter-free kitchen, adding to the sense of space.

Another kind of connectedness resulted from the wife's desire to keep parts of the old kitchen to which she had grown attached. Just because they were building a new kitchen, she didn't feel they had to throw out everything. Having lived with and loved certain aspects of her old kitchen, she asked the architect to reuse the pro-style range, the pot rack that hangs from the ceiling, the light fixtures above the island, and the library-style, swing-arm lamps on the desk. Retaining some of their favorite elements gave this modern space a sense of comfort and personality.

upclose

1 Tray storage cabinets

t o get a lot out of a little space, this kitchen uses a few clever tricks.

1 Among the many handy storage features integrated into this cabinet system are the tray cabinets on either side of the stove.

2 A pair of refrigerator drawers not only provides additional cold storage space but also makes wine, vegetables, and other ingredients easily accessible to cooks preparing food at the island.

3 The desk sits between the working center of the kitchen and the sitting area and serves as a multipurpose surface for everything from reading to entertaining.

4 Clad in the same finish as the rest of the cabinets in the kitchen, the pantry cabinet is virtually invisible until you open it up to reveal two well-stuffed racks of storage.

2 Refrigerator
drawers

3 Desk

4 Pantry
cabinet

"A workhorse of a rental that was beyond run-down"

An old-fashioned kitchen loaded with modern amenities

tHE KITCHEN OF JASON PORTER'S Oakland, California, apartment was the result of a renovation that combined four small apartments in a landmark Victorian building into one large, two-story unit. From the start, Jason knew that he wanted the space to have more in common with the original 1870 home than it did with the well-worn kitchen it replaced. The once-magnificent structure was a single-family home before being subdivided 100 years ago into small apartments. While Jason respected the historic nature of the building, he didn't want (nor could he afford) to re-create a grand Victorian confection. His goal was a well-functioning kitchen, no bigger than it needed to be, which possessed a style that lay somewhere between period reproduction and modern efficiency. An important part of his plan was to use fresh, lively colors that would be in keeping with the past.

Bringing in the Light

Since the kitchen faced south, Jason also wanted it to take advantage of the sunlight. There was just a

AFTER

A careful mix of classic design, sunshine, and bright color gives this traditional kitchen an infusion of style and elegance that makes it the centerpiece of its newly remodeled home.

BEFORE

The original kitchen, covered with dark blue tile, was fitted with basic equipment that was far beyond its prime and added to the room's dinginess.

out of sight

■ By adding a roll-out shelf, the storage area above the refrigerator becomes an ideal place to stow light appliances that are seldom used. The small, 60-in.-high refrigerator makes this an easily accessible storage solution, which it might not be in a kitchen with a tall refrigerator. Here the shelf is a clever use of underutilized space.

quickfixes

When redesigning a vintage kitchen, consider mixing original details and historic woodwork with state-of-the-art appliances to give your kitchen a feeling of richness and authority.

utilitarian kitchen window to brighten the room. As was the fashion in its day, the kitchen had been walled off from the dining room with nothing but a single door passing between them. As a result, the dining room was even darker. One of Jason's primary goals was to redesign the kitchen so that it and the remaining interior living spaces received as much light as possible.

Jason's renovation plan, which was developed with architect Michael Mullin of San Francisco, was to extend the kitchen into space previously occupied by a bathroom, stretching the 12-ft.-long kitchen to 17 ft. At the same time, Mullin designed exterior windows and a glass door leading out to the deck. On the newly extended interior wall, Mullin added a second doorway, and at

above This new triple window replaced the original single one. The faucet is a 100-year-old design that is still made by the manufacturer—proof of its enduring style.

facing page A new deck and glass door leading to it extend the kitchen into the sunny outdoors. A transom window above the door enhances the connection.

the other end of the kitchen, he took the existing door off its frame. The kitchen now had two entrances but no heavy doors blocking the sun. In addition, Mullin added a wide pass-through to the dining room that not only functions as a convenient way to serve food but also allows the sunlight to flood into the whole apartment. The result is a kitchen that works as a transition from the outdoors to the dining/living area instead of being the barrier that it had once been.

Jason also hired a professional color consultant to work out the palette he would use in the kitchen and dining room. Together Jason and the designer came up with a color scheme that matched the traditional style of the kitchen but would register with modern eyes. The dominant color they chose is a classic shade of blue that

left Pale yellow and blue tones are the perfect complement to the crisp white crown molding, extra-wide baseboards, and trim details in this Victorian apartment.

before & after

The old kitchen, designed for a one-bedroom rental unit, was too small, closed off, and dark. Despite its southern exposure, a single small window cut the bright sunshine to a minimum. In addition to annexing space from a bathroom, the architect added a glass doorway to the outside and an interior pass-through that lets light in.

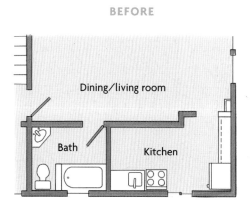

BEFORE

Dining/living room

Bath

Kitchen

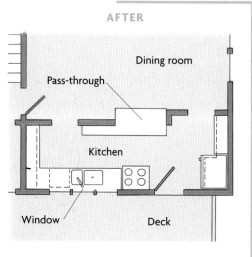

AFTER

Dining room

Pass-through

Kitchen

Window

Deck

hints at times past and was derived from the blue-gray of the flooring. A slightly darker shade was used for the base cabinets and the open shelving and then was cut with white paint to lighten it for the upper cabinets. This trick of shifting shades gives the base cabinets more heft and grounding, while it makes the upper cabinets seem lighter and less imposing. Even paler shades of this blue appear in the backsplash tiles. The walls are painted with fresh pale yellow that adds light to the small space.

Jason's new stainless-steel appliances, including the pro-style 30-in. range, dishwasher, vent hood, and refrigerator, add to the room's fresh, contemporary quality.

A Pleasing Mix

Trendy appliances aside, the new kitchen is stylistically a happy throwback to older, calmer times. The spare, custom-crafted cabinets are hand-painted with alkyd paint to give them a vintage sensibility. The upper cabinets are fitted with reeded glass doors that add to the feeling. Wherever possible, the original trim and detailing were maintained; where new molding and details were created, they were designed to match the originals.

Another nod to vintage style is the kitchen floor, which is covered in Marmoleum®, an affordable flooring product made just as it was 100 years ago from all-natural linseed oil, rosin (dried pine sap), chalk, wood flour, and jute backing. After disappearing in the 1960s, linoleum has been rediscovered, not only because it is considered an environmentally friendly product but also because it hearkens back to the kitchens of our grandparents' era. It comes in 7-ft.-wide

Working with Pros

ESSENTIAL STEP

Assuming the role of general contractor, Jason Porter hired a construction crew, a cabinetmaker, a color consultant, an electrician, and a plumber. He did this in part to control the flow of money (in fact, he didn't save much) but also to be more directly involved in the process. He paid many on an hourly basis, a formula sometimes used for projects in old construction where accurate estimates are difficult but which can open up a homeowner to runaway costs. This system worked for Jason because he was able to tap into a network of young craftspeople who were less expensive and able to work to Jason's standards. There was only one negative: The role took up an inordinate amount of time. In the future, Jason says, he would treat it as a full-time job.

sheets, like what is used here, or as tiles for patterned floors, and it can be found through flooring retailers.

The mix of the old and new that grew out of this blend of carefully considered restoration, imaginative reinterpretation, and flat-out modern machinery has created a kitchen that is as eye-catching as it is comfortable and cozy.

upclose

1 Swing-out corner storage

above With the help of a color consultant, the kitchen and dining room were transformed into bright, charming spaces.

To fit a lot of utility into this small space, Jason used a combination of simple, old-fashioned storage solutions and clever new design tricks.

1 The hard-to-reach corner recess behind the dishwasher is turned into an efficient storage area with this swing-out rack system.

2 The reeded glass on the front of the cabinets discreetly hides the contents but, at the same time, gives the cabinets lightness and translucency.

3 Shallow open shelves below the pass-through are a perfect spot for storing spices and condiments without taking much space.

2 Glass-front cabinet

3 Open shelving

"An ordinary kitchen in an extraordinary location"

THE SOLUTION

A cook's paradise with spectacular views

THE KITCHEN OF ART LEACH AND JUDY HENNESSY'S Jackson, Wyoming, home is surrounded by spectacular scenery. Unfortunately, like many speculative-built houses, this one was constructed from a cookie-cutter plan that virtually ignored the views of the nearby Teton Mountains. Since both of their professional lives revolved around food and the original kitchen was as basic as the house, Art and Judy budgeted for a renovation right from the start. Art, a chef and restaurant owner, and Judy, a certified nutritionist, loved to have large groups over for dinner. Then, three years ago, when Art decided to conduct cooking classes in their home, their renovation plans took on a specific urgency.

The couple decided to create a whole new kitchen, one that was more spacious as well as worthy of its setting with wide-open windows to pull in the mountain views. Their new cooking, teaching, and entertaining space would need to be designed to allow 20 or more people watch Art prepare food.

AFTER

The kitchen of this redesigned builder's spec home is open to the mountains in the distance as well as to the friends and family close at hand. A massive overhead beam opens the space up while wrapping the kitchen in its warm embrace.

BEFORE

The old kitchen featured an interesting metallic backsplash but was otherwise too out-of-the-box for these serious cooks.

very personal pizza

■ One of the most delightful features of this kitchen is the wood-burning oven. Since it was not much more expensive than a standard wall oven, Art and Judy considered it a modest splurge at most. The fire is built right in the cooking chamber, and as anyone who has eaten pizza or bread baked this way will tell you, the flavor is exceptional. The oven is a preassembled oven by Earthstone®, a California company that specializes in wood-fired ovens for residential and commercial use. But wood-fired ovens are also available in less-expensive unassembled kits. In any case, the oven must be insulated for home use and requires a dedicated 6-in. to 8-in. chimney for ventilation.

Kitchen as Theater

It's not every client who comes to an architect with the task of creating a kitchen that can handle cooking classes and intimate meals for two, plus capitalize on its gorgeous natural surroundings. The challenge before architect Stephen Dynia was partly structural, partly visual. First, he designed a massive crossbeam to replace the former exterior bearing wall that supported the roof at this end of the house. Spanning the space under the high ceilings, this beam also became an important design element, creating a proscenium arch over this kitchen and turning the everyday cooking area into a performance space. It also created an important visual boundary between the kitchen and the dining area.

above With four burners, a griddle, a grill, and two ovens, the range is ready to take on any cooking challenge. A high-capacity vent hood is needed to handle the heat and grilling smoke.

above A stainless-steel-covered island draws the eye even when the kitchen is empty, but it becomes center stage for Art Leach's cooking classes as he prepares his signature dishes.

Making It Happen

The first thing Art Leach and Judy Hennessy asked for in the new design was to bring the views of the Teton Mountains deep into the space so that they could enjoy them from virtually any place in the kitchen. The second need was to create a space flexible enough to accommodate big parties, group cooking classes, small dinners, and casual, private meals. Structurally, this meant designing an open space with lots of windows and without any interior walls that would obstruct potential sight lines. Architect Stephen Dynia's solution was a large laminated crossbeam that supports two smaller cantilevered beams. These in turn support the roof and leave the interior open. The resulting exposed arch emerged as the focal point of the room as well as an ideal place to install bright lights to illuminate the island.

Ease and Efficiency

Theatric intentions aside, the basic design of the kitchen itself is simple. The new kitchen space is conceived as a shallow U surrounding a long, stainless-steel-covered island, which is spacious enough to spread out a sumptuous meal for 12 guests or several demonstration dishes for students. Along the back is a wall of enormous picture windows extending up to the roof that are interrupted by just a few appliances.

Art wanted the working part of the kitchen to be an easy place to cook with equipment that is state of the art but with everything simply designed and convenient. To that end, the kitchen is fitted with professional-style appliances, including a wood-fired wall oven and a 48-in.-wide stainless-steel gas range with four burners, a grill, a griddle, and two ovens. Because Art wanted to avoid the stringent code requirements that come with professional equipment, which tends to operate at higher temperatures, he installed residential-grade appliances. He added studded rubber flooring that is common in restaurant kitchens because it is soft on feet and easy to clean.

Everything needed for cooking is easy to reach. Pots are hung overhead, and the shelves beneath the counters hold equipment, utensils, and dishware. A pantry on one side of the kitchen takes care of deep storage for extra staples for Art's classes as well as seldom-used cooking equipment.

Unique Multipurpose Table

The key element of the whole design is a movable oval tabletop that fits into a slot in the island and that quickly switches functions. When the table is in the slot, it becomes a long bar that serves as an intimate dining spot for the couple when they are alone or as the stage for Art's cooking classes. When the table is pulled out, it can be dressed up as a formal dining table. This flexibility

above A compact pantry closet provides storage for seldom-used kitchen appliances and staples for cooking classes.

left A spacious pantry tucked into an alcove at one end of the kitchen holds many of the couple's cooking necessities, such as a bread maker, standing mixer, and food processor. A mini-refrigerator keeps bottles from the wine cellar chilled.

before & after

The layout of the old kitchen squeezed all of the activity onto a small L-shaped counter and cut the kitchen off from the views. The new kitchen has the room and, thanks to the large island, the work space to perform the full range of activities the couple uses it for.

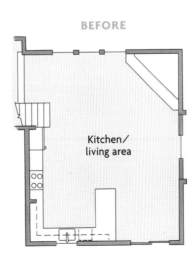

BEFORE

Kitchen/ living area

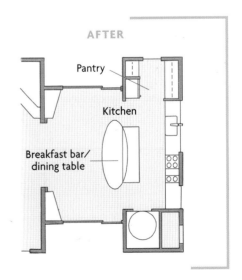

AFTER

Pantry

Kitchen

Breakfast bar/ dining table

OUR BIG SPLURGE

movable feasts

■ The one element that defines this kitchen is the custom-built movable table that slides in and out of the island, transforming it from casual breakfast bar to formal dining table. This versatility helps the space work both professionally and personally for the couple. By combining functions in one cleverly furnished piece of furniture, architect Stephen Dynia made optimum use of the limited floor space in this single-story house. The 8-ft.-long, oblong, cherry table fits into a deep slot along the front of the island to become a curved bar facing the kitchen and the views beyond. It can then be pulled away from the island (with legs attached) for use as a dining table.

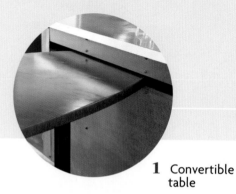

1 Convertible table

the crossbeam over the island serves to create a stage area where Art can perform his magic with food for students and dinner guests.

1 The slot in the island easily accepts this innovative, dual-purpose table/breakfast bar.

2 Monopoint lights set along the overhead beam are controlled by dimmers to accommodate different room functions.

3 Studded rubber flooring from a home center and open shelves are two design features borrowed from restaurant kitchens.

4 Bread and pizza cooked right in the firebox of the wood oven deliver a sublime smoky taste.

eliminates the need for a separate dining room and conserves valuable floor space in this modest-sized house.

This kitchen is a skillful blend of showmanship and efficiency. However, the whole design is compact enough that when the theater lights go down, Art and Judy can make themselves very much at home.

2 Overhead lighting

3 Rubber flooring

4 Wood oven

lighting the way

above Recessed lights arrayed around the edge of the kitchen keep the countertop work areas well lit and safe by day, while under-cabinet lights assist after dark.

LIGHTING IS ONE OF THE MOST IMPORTANT and often overlooked aspects of kitchen design. At a minimum, it is a safety factor. The combination of hot foods, sharp knives, and poorly lit counters is a dangerous one. But lighting also directly affects the enjoyment of your kitchen. When done improperly and inadequately, it will reduce your ability to use the entire space as you designed it. When done well, though, lighting can lift a merely good kitchen into the realm of the sensational.

The first consideration of any good lighting plan is to understand how the natural light coming through windows, skylights, glass doors, and other spaces works its way around your kitchen throughout the day. The more you are able to use and direct this light with light-colored surfaces, strategic openings, or even mirrors, the less you will have to use artificial light.

Since the sun eventually sets (for those of us living below the Arctic Circle), having the right combination of lighting sources throughout a kitchen is essential. The three general types are ambient, task, and accent lighting. These should be layered throughout the kitchen so functions and coverage overlap.

right These reproduction Victorian fixtures provide subtle overhead light and lots of style for this period renovation in Vermont.

Ambient Lighting

As the name implies, this is atmosphere lighting. It can be created with recessed lights, wall sconces, pendant lights, track lights, chandeliers, or some combination of these.

Task Lighting

This is lighting for areas like countertops, islands, and cooking surfaces. It should be bright, widespread, and installed at close intervals to minimize shadows. Where

left Well-spaced recessed ceiling lights keep every corner of this small kitchen bathed in bright light, while a pair of pendant lights illuminates the work island in the middle.

below This inexpensive wall sconce with a white wrap-around diffusing shade scatters light through 180 degrees of space, while its simple chic design creates its own stylistic bright spot.

there are upper cabinets, hidden under-cabinet lighting is a good way to light counters. Over islands and peninsulas, directed recess lights can be used, but pendant lights bring the light down to work level.

Accent Lighting

To light up the decorative features, architecture, or objects you love, scatter accent lights around the kitchen in the form of directed spotlights.

Once you've completed your lighting scheme, make sure that the lights can be controlled with dimmable switches. This lets you fine-tune the total light experience in your kitchen for each situation, i.e., low ambient light with select task and accent lighting partly on for entertaining, or everything on all the way for homework or breakfast.

"Darkness when there should have been light"

Lots of windows and drawers, lots of light and space

bEFORE JIM AND NORMA SPRADLING decided to remodel the kitchen of their 1971 contemporary house, they had lived in it for 30 years. In that time, they had become grudgingly accustomed to its limited size, low ceilings, and poor light. By the standards of sunny Los Altos, California, where they live, theirs was a decidedly dark kitchen. Facing east with low, overhanging eaves, the kitchen received some brief morning light and then slid into the shadows for the rest of the day. In 2003, after being posted by Jim's corporation to Munich, Germany, for three years, the couple came home knowing they needed a change. They wanted a new kitchen that not only resolved all of the old problems of insufficient height, space, and light but also was as efficient as the one they'd had in Germany.

Finding Abundant Light

To attack this ambitious new plan, they hired Los Altos architect Peter Duxbury, and the first thing Duxbury did was open the space up. He moved the eastern exterior wall out four feet, consuming a small portion of the

AFTER

A full-sized, 48-in.-wide professional-style range defines this light and airy kitchen as a no-nonsense work space.

BEFORE

Dark wood cabinets compounded the effect of the low ceilings, undersized windows, and overhanging eaves to make the old kitchen a drab space.

Making It Happen

Once Jim and Norma had worked out the general style and layout of their kitchen with Duxbury, they had to sort through the myriad finishing details. High among their concerns was how to organize the cabinets to maximize both storage and convenience within the space. The couple urged Duxbury to design a lot of small, easily compartmentalized drawer spaces to make storing and finding tools and uten-

sils easy. They ended up with 62 drawers in this modest-sized kitchen, including a pair of refrigerator drawers. All of the cabinets are fitted with roll-out shelves, allowing cooking utensils to come to you rather than the other way around. The one exception to this pull-out storage strategy is the pantry closet, where Duxbury designed a series of fixed U-shaped shelves so that everything from the top to the bottom is both well lit and easily accessible.

quickfixes

A stepped-down eating area built onto the end of the island creates a gathering space that is close by but separate.

couple's large deck. This change resulted in a higher roof line, which he left open to the rafters to eliminate the problematic low ceiling. He also removed a wall that separated the kitchen from a nearby pantry and incorporated the pantry space into the kitchen. Finally, he turned the former breakfast room, which had previously adjoined the kitchen, into a part of a grand, new family room. He separated this space from the kitchen with a high wall that runs to the peak of the roof. The upshot of all of these changes is not only a kitchen that is literally quite a bit bigger than the original but also one that gives the illusion of much more space than its modest 12-ft. by 14-ft. dimensions might suggest.

To produce the abundant light that the couple wanted, Duxbury added lots of new windows. He punctuated the sloping roof above the kitchen with two sets of three 3-ft. by 4-ft. skylights: One set is placed along the peak, reflecting light off the new high wall, while another set is located along the eaves line, lighting up the counters on the morning side of the kitchen. Behind these counters, he placed two wide windows that yield to two

facing page Wide picture windows behind the counters and large skylights above ensure that this space remains intimately connected to the sunny outdoors.

left A pair of clerestory windows at the peak of the new roof adds to the sense of openness and light.

above To break up the monolithic effect of the solid wall of cabinets, the architect placed open display shelves along the top, which adds texture and depth while giving the eye a reprieve from the flatness of the surfaces below.

microwave in a box

■ Although many of us are used to the reality of a microwave staring at us whenever we enter our kitchens, it doesn't have to be that way. A disappearing microwave is a simple thing to accomplish. While the remedy here, a hydraulically assisted lifting door, is especially high tech, less ambitious strategies are available, such as simple cabinet doors or pull-down tambour doors. Keep in mind that the doors need to be left open while operating the microwave to allow any heat to dissipate.

large sliding glass doors that open onto the deck. Finally, he added a pair of clerestory windows at the peak of the high ceiling to bring in still more light.

To enhance this feeling of lightness and space, Duxbury wrapped the kitchen in white walls and pale, flat maple cabinets with simple, no-nonsense hardware that bounce the light around the space. Matching light maple floors add to the effect.

Making Space

To bring efficiency to this soaring space, Duxbury created a simple plan: a long, bilevel island surrounded by four walls covered almost completely with cabinetry, which also helped to replace storage space that was lost by the annexation of the

left The high walls of the kitchen reflect the plentiful sunshine from the skylights and help fill the space with light, while the abundant storage keeps the space uncluttered.

before & after

The old layout created a long, narrow space oriented toward a breakfast room that was rarely used and had a large but inefficient pantry. The small dining table added to the new island allowed the home-owners to turn the under-used breakfast room into a family room.

BEFORE

Breakfast room

Family room

Dining room

Kitchen

Deck

Pantry

AFTER

Deck

Family room

Dining room

Kitchen

Island

pantry. The storage in these cabinets is mostly in the form of highly efficient drawers—62 of them in all. Norma, an emergency-room nurse who is used to having supplies and instruments within easy reach, prefers drawers to cabinets with doors because drawers allow her to retrieve tools quickly.

The Island

A central part of the design is an island topped with honed black granite with a butcher-block breakfast table set at one end, which replaces, in much less space, the former breakfast room. The island was designed with two levels to handle all types of activity, from preparing a salad to reading the paper. At one end sits a 6-ft. by 4-ft. black granite work area; at the other is a 3-ft. by 4-ft. butcher-block extension. Situated near the range and refrigerator, the upper level is part of the working kitchen and equipped with a small prep sink. The table extension, located away from the business end of the kitchen, is a standard table height of 30 inches, making it an ideal place for leisurely coffee breaks or to serve food when the couple entertains.

The granite backsplashes provide an easy-to-clean, reflective surface behind the counters. Since both of the Spradlings are avid cooks, they chose high-quality, state-of-the-art appliances: a six-burner, pro-style range topped by a wide stainless hood and vent; a wide, side-by-side, built-in refrigerator; and a second sink on the island so they can both work in the kitchen without getting in each other's way.

The resulting combination of light, space, efficiency, and cooking capacity has delivered a hard-working yet beautiful kitchen that is a pleasure to work in and a delight to live in.

upclose

1 Slotted pantry shelves

bigger windows, higher ceilings, and skylights brighten the new kitchen and make it a more pleasurable place to spend time.

1 U-shaped shelves in the pantry cabinet were designed to allow light to reach all of the shelves; the design also makes it easy to retrieve stored objects.

2 Two refrigerator drawers in the island add cooling capacity and keep ingredients close to the prep area.

3 A bank of skylights along the east-facing roof line allows the morning light to pour in.

4 A small desk designed into the far wall of cabinets does double duty as an espresso station.

2 Refrigerator drawers

3 Skylights

4 Little desk

"A dark kitchen shoehorned into leftover space"

Opening walls created a charming cooking center

AFTER

The owners of this tiny kitchen got a lot for their money by opening up walls. The shape of the arched pass-through echoes the shape of the window in the dining room, connecting the two rooms visually and capturing natural light.

FOR 20 YEARS, ED SINGER AND ELLEN VINE had lived with the small kitchen of their Berkeley, California, home, painting over the old wood cabinets and then repainting them every few years. But their kitchen had problems that new paint wouldn't fix. Although the original 1920s California Craftsman-style house had a lot of charm, numerous renovations over its history had resulted in a patchwork of little rooms and ad hoc spaces that were walled off from each other and the rest of the house. Because of the layout, the sunshine that poured into a hallway next to the kitchen barely filtered into the kitchen's inner recesses.

Poor layout aside, the old kitchen looked its age. The laminate countertops were peeling, and the many layers of paint had grown a little thick. After coping with the kitchen's idiosyncrasies for what they felt was long enough, the couple was ready to remodel and to bring in some light and fresh fixtures. They wanted to open up the kitchen, but not too much because, given their tiny lot, there was no space for expansion.

BEFORE

The many renovations that formed the old kitchen left features such as this quirky partial wall that served only to create shade on the inside of the space.

Taking Stock

Ed and Ellen had lived with their old kitchen for 20 years, more than long enough to understand what worked and what didn't. The kitchen had always felt too dark and closed in; it was blocked off from the rest of the house and, most importantly, from the large windows in the hallway and dining room that poured light into the adjoining rooms. The cabinet styles had grown ever more out of date, while the cracked and peeling laminate counters showed sure signs of their ample age. The couple had spruced up the kitchen from time to time with a coat of bright paint on the old wooden cabinets, but they now knew that it would take a complete remodel to address the kitchen's many basic spatial and organizational problems.

Ordering the Chaos

To bring order to the hodgepodge of rooms, they hired Berkeley architect Dennis Fox. Their mandate to him was to design a kitchen that was new in terms of style, features, and equipment but not in-your-face contemporary. They also hoped to make the space brighter and more connected to the rest of the house and to add a breakfast nook.

Since all of this newness had to happen in a limited amount of space, together they moved around walls and counters on paper until they came up with a plan that would give Ed and Ellen what they wanted. This exercise helped them visualize the myriad variations, along with the pluses and minuses of each. In the end, they decided the kitchen should expand into the nearby dining room, making good use of an odd wedge of space.

Although the new kitchen design produced no additional counter space, Fox was able, by using several creative tricks, to add a considerable amount of storage space. Newly available gadgets such as a two-stage pull-out shelf system rescued lost space from one deep corner of the cabinets. Fox also invented his own low-tech storage solutions like the 3-ft.-deep drawers that access another dead corner from the far side of the cabinets. An efficient custom-designed pantry cabinet below the microwave added still more storage.

Breaking Through

The new design added a great deal of light—both natural and otherwise. An old half-wall was removed, producing not only more light but enough room for a table and chairs. In addition, Fox designed a large pass-through between the kitchen and dining room, echoing the shape of the arched picture window in the dining room and brightening the kitchen considerably.

above A small television is installed on a swiveling, pull-out shelf so it can be viewed from the table during breakfast or snacks or stowed during homework time.

left The cozy breakfast table and bench sit in a once-dead hall space—one of the bonuses of removing an inconvenient wall. The other bonus is more natural light.

before & after

In the old plan, an overzealous commitment to having a square kitchen left lots of nearby space underused. By breaking out of the box and using a creative new layout, the architect was able to bring badly needed space into the kitchen from unexpected places.

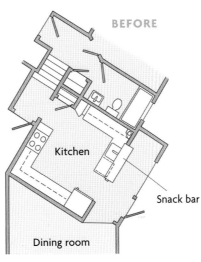

BEFORE

Kitchen

Snack bar

Dining room

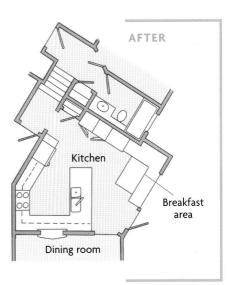

AFTER

Kitchen

Breakfast area

Dining room

layers of light

■ As any good kitchen should be, this one is equipped with different types of lights. Architect Dennis Fox designed ambient, task, and accent lighting to provide flexible coverage for all of the kitchen's activities. The ambient lighting, which helps

define background light levels, comes from eight recessed lights that flood the entire area. Task lighting to make the countertop work areas bright and safe comes in the form of under-cabinet strip lighting, while a series of white glass pendant lamps provide task lighting over the peninsula and the breakfast table. Spotlights directed onto the glass shelves on the wall and the wooden shelves accent the objects displayed there.

Stylistically, the kitchen is neither too contemporary nor especially traditional. The spare, framed cabinets are made of light maple, and the countertops are polished black granite. While the kitchen has been fitted with lots of Craftsman-like details, features such as the stainless range, vent hood, and refrigerator place it clearly in the present.

By borrowing a small amount of space from the dining room, being clever about how they arranged the entire space, and using innovative design details, Ed and Ellen have created a sweet—yet hardworking—haven in their busy house.

upclose

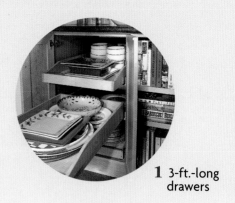

1 3-ft.-long drawers

the compact design of this kitchen not only allows for creative storage space but also for beautiful and practical architectural features, like this pass-through into the dining room.

1 These 3-ft.-long drawers offer an alternative solution for storing bulky platters and trays.

2 High-efficiency features like this European-designed, two-stage pull-out shelving system used to access a deep corner space help the couple get the most out of their modest space.

3 This rack pulls out partway for quick-storage items and further for deep storage.

4 A series of glass-shaded pendant lights above the island add light and create a delightful sculptural effect.

2 Sliding
storage

3 Double
drawer

4 Pendant
lights

"It was like cooking in a closet"

The heart of the home and sunlight, too

THE OWNER OF THIS 1930S SPANISH REVIVAL farmhouse high in the hills of Berkeley, California, had one wish: to make her kitchen the place within her home where everyone would gravitate—friends and family alike. The kitchen she and her husband found when they bought the home was a rambling and constricted space, not much more than an elaborate hallway, as dismal as it was inefficient. Knowing that she and her family spent a big chunk of their lives in the kitchen, she wanted the new one to be a place that reflected the informal California lifestyle they lived as well as the easygoing yet sophisticated cuisine that they loved to cook for friends. And she desired a touch of drama.

The design that they and Berkeley architect Hiro Morimoto came up with extended the kitchen both up and out, resulting in a space that was much lighter, airier, and decidedly more striking. To add a small amount of floor space, the side exterior wall of the kitchen was moved out 5 ft., while the rear exterior wall was extended 8 ft., adding somewhat to the cost of the project but allowing the couple to trade a few square feet of outdoor driveway

AFTER

Cozy comforts such as the bright breakfast nook with its Mexican-style table and hanging lamp and natural finishes like granite, tile, and copper used in the main cooking area bring balance to the new design.

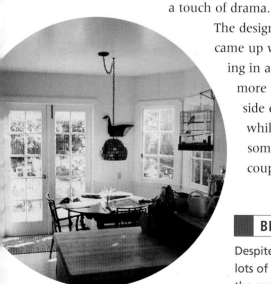

BEFORE

Despite the fact that the original kitchen received lots of sunlight, its low ceilings and small size made the space cramped and uninviting.

Making It Happen

As with any person you meet, a kitchen that has personality is a kitchen you want to know better. In this kitchen, the homeowners and architect Hiro Morimoto have done just that. They've created a space that is layered and complex, with subtle details yet a definite liveliness, the kind of kitchen you want to spend time in. They have done this mostly with the many finishing touches, which include not only large design elements like the copper vent hood but also the many barely noticeable details such as the copper leading in the cabinets that echoes the copper in the hood, the rounded plaster corners of the walls, the carefully crafted cupboards, the hand-glazed tiles around the cooktop, and the movable cabinets on either side of the island.

above Choosing a cooktop over a standard range translates into having more room for pot storage underneath, and a griddle and six burners mean fewer hassles when cooking for a crowd.

space for a kitchen that was large enough to suit their needs and a breakfast nook that could handle more than a couple of people.

Crafting the Focal Point

Visually anchoring the center of the new kitchen is a large sculptural vent hood that hangs above a cooking island. The copper vent, which was given a patina to make it look old and rustic, serves as a sort of exclamation point that defines this as the hardworking heart of the kitchen.

The cooking island is equipped with a professional-style, six-burner cooktop and is trimmed with handmade green tiles that bring a touch of craftsmanship to this hi-tech appliance. On either side of the island is a pair of small, movable cabinets topped with dark green granite designed as freestanding furniture pieces that can be moved into new positions as needed.

On the opposite side of the island from the sink are a pair of wall ovens and a small counter

above Because these two wall ovens stand slightly apart from the rest of the cooking area, the architect created a work niche that serves as a handy staging area for food coming in or out of the ovens.

cedar ceiling

■ To add a unique touch to the kitchen without adding greatly to the cost, the contractor paneled the ceiling with hard-to-find Port Orford cedar planks, a durable wood that is only grown along a small section of the Oregon coast. Among the hardest of

the softwoods, this cedar is a pale, creamy color with a fine, straight grain, making it an ideal wood for interior finishes. It has a pleasant, distinctive ginger smell and is insect resistant, so it is sometimes used for lining clothes closets. While it was chosen here because of its light color and rich, tight-grained appearance, its durability also lends itself well to a high-humidity location such as a kitchen. The contractor, Tom Alderson, luckily managed to find a batch of rough lumber that didn't cost too much and had it milled into ³⁄₈-in.-thick planks to make the small amount stretch further.

niche to provide a place to put food going in and out of the ovens. To the right of the ovens, the architect created a snug pantry closet that fits perfectly under a staircase.

Finding Color and Light

The color scheme of the kitchen has been kept intentionally light and neutral to allow the space and its natural brightness to stand on its own. With the exception of the dark green granite used to top the side cabinets of the island and on the backsplashes, most of the finishes in the kitchen and breakfast nook are pale and creamy white. The maple and poplar cabinets are left in their light, natural state with minimal finish, and the top of the L-shaped counters are done in simple white Corian, which the homeowner preferred aesthetically to dark granite in this part of the kitchen and which cost significantly less. She also liked the way the different countertop colors defined each zone of the kitchen. In the end, the relative absence of strong color also adds to the relaxed, uncluttered feel of the design.

before&after

The old floor plan was not at all conducive to hanging out. The new plan has nearly doubled the size of the kitchen and streamlined the way the space is arranged so that family and guests can gather and stay.

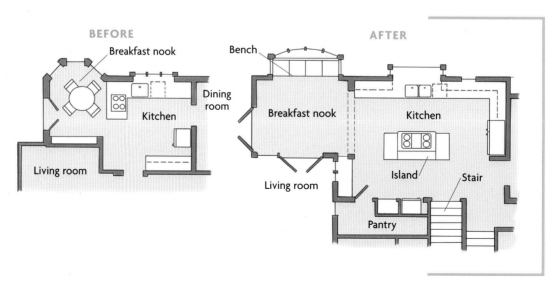

Crowning the space is a ceiling of hard-to-find Port Orford cedar, a very light-colored and fine-grained wood that adds to the natural ease of the space. The wood, which is slightly more expensive than regular cedar, was cut into thin ⅜-in.-thick panels to keep this particular splurge within the budget.

Adding Rustic Details

For the floor, the homeowners chose traditional, widely available, and inexpensive terra-cotta tiles from Mexico, which enhance the rustic feeling they wanted. Another detail that adds to the roughly finished character of the space are the handblown glass panes with tiny bubbles used in the doors of the upper cabinets, which are also held in place by delicate copper leading to match the copper of the vent hood. Bubble glass is another inexpensive option, also produced in Mexico and readily available through cabinet-supply houses for little more than the cost of clear glass. On the other hand, the copper leading was a bit of a splurge but added a fine finish that contrasts beautifully with the rustic touches. The

ADDED INGREDIENTS

space-saving pantry

■ The presence of a staircase along one side of the kitchen resulted in an empty space that Morimoto used to create a pantry closet, reducing the need for more storage cabinets in

the kitchen itself. Shallow shelves along the back wall are just the right depth for canned and packaged goods. A deeper half-height set of shelves on the right leaves space for a counter on top that can be used to store large cookware or small appliances like a juicer or a standing mixer. Morimoto cut a small window above this counter to allow sunlight to flood in, making this a great place to keep baskets of ripening fruits and vegetables.

roomy new breakfast nook is fitted with a Mexican-style table and chairs that sit under a modern light fixture with a punched-tin shade, all of which add to the down-to-earth yet distinctive feeling of this kitchen.

Together, all of these elements add up to exactly the sort of space that the homeowners wanted, a kitchen that is casual enough to work as the vital center of the household where the family lingers in comfort but elegant enough to be the unmistakable gathering place for large groups of friends.

1 Hidden dishwasher

the floor area around the island was intentionally designed with room for a crowd. Here the distance between the island and counter is nearly 5 ft., considerably more than the recommended minimum of 42 in.

1 The dishwasher is hidden behind a wood panel to maintain the clean lines of the custom maple cabinets.

2 A handy pop-up storage shelf allows quick access to the food processor, which can just as easily be stowed.

3 Instead of being covered up, this small, shallow recess above the refrigerator was turned into an elegant display niche for showing off antique baskets and boxes.

4 Deep and wide drawers installed underneath the cooktop keep necessary pots and pans at the ready.

2 Pop-up
storage shelf

3 Display storage
niche

4 Pot storage
drawers

"A funky 1970s renovation"

A beautiful bungalow update that uses every inch of space

AFTER

Because the design of this modest-sized kitchen emphasizes the efficient and ordered use of space, it delivers far more function than many kitchens its size.

THE KITCHEN THAT CAME with Stephanie Rubinoff's Moorish-style bungalow in the hills of Oakland, California, had little to do with the rest of the house. It was the creation of an ill-conceived renovation dating from the 1970s that turned the small galley kitchen into a dark and cramped labyrinth of badly laid out cabinets. The rest of the 1930s vintage house, by comparison, recalled a more elegant past when craft and character were an integral part of home design. The moment she moved in, she set about redoing the kitchen into a more usable space that would be built with the same level of quality, if not in the same style, as the rest of the house.

Stephanie's primary goal for her renovation was to open up and reorganize the kitchen, which was a virtual obstacle course of dark, old-fashioned cupboards. She knew that given the size of her yard as well as cost and zoning restraints, she would have to do this without adding space or expanding outward. To accomplish the heavy construction, she hired

BEFORE

Dark, awkwardly placed cabinets and an intrusive peninsula cut up the available space into small, unusable pieces.

Working with Pros

Stephanie's contractor suggested she use a kitchen designer and recommended Jennie Gisslow, CKD, of Design Source, who is certified by the National Kitchen and Bath Association with expertise in products, codes, and design. She designed the finished floor plan, came up with a detailed cabinet scheme, helped Stephanie choose the appliances, and suggested such finishes as the slate floors and backsplash, the red birch cabinets, and the honed granite countertops. If design is important and you know your project requires no complicated structural alterations, hiring a certified kitchen designer can be an effective decision and a less expensive alternative to using an architect.

Keith Alward, an award-winning local contractor. To help with design details, Alward referred her to kitchen designer Jennie Gisslow of Design Source in nearby San Leandro. The result is a fresh, well-equipped space that is connected visually and aesthetically to the rest of the house.

Hidden Extras

Instead of a zigzag obstacle course, the layout is now that of a galley kitchen with two counters facing each other along a long, narrow space. The counters, cabinets, and appliances are far more rationally laid out, so that the space flows into and through the kitchen more freely, carrying one from the dining room on one side out onto the patio in back.

What's more, the cabinets in the kitchen are designed to exploit every opportunity for storage yet are no bigger than necessary, which is especially important in a modest-sized, tightly arranged kitchen. Among the many novel storage solutions that Gisslow designed into the cabinets was a shallow 3-in. space, just wide enough for spice jars and condiments, that she created for the leftover space around a chimney flue. Also, at two points in the kitchen where square cabinets would not fit without impeding traffic flow, she designed diagonal cabinets, each capable of holding dozens of cans.

facing page The small integrated table/peninsula anchors one end of the kitchen without crowding the layout, creating a useful spot to grab a quick meal or linger over a cup of tea.

shades of slate

■ Slate tiles are a good choice for kitchen floors, where a soft, rugged, and casual feel is desired. Since slate is a porous rock, though, it needs to be sealed on installation and resealed every couple of years, as do any grout lines. Slate is available in a wide range of earth tones, from soft gray to green to rust, and in several finishes. The tiles used here came in premixed batches in an assortment of colors and shades. It pays to spend time playing with patterns and combinations of tile colors, first on paper and then with full-sized colored templates, before trying to move around real tiles. The designer and client here made full-sized color photocopies of several standard shades so they could easily move the colors around and work out patterns for both the floor and the backsplashes.

quickfixes

Removing doors from passageways where they are no longer useful (such as the old swinging door between the kitchen and dining room) or substituting pocket doors for conventional doors can help open up a small space.

Adding Texture

Although Stephanie did not want the kitchen to mimic the vintage style of the house, she did want it to reflect the spirit and quality of the home's original construction. To achieve these ends, Gisslow used red birch wood for the cabinets because it has the rich appearance of cherry but is not as dark, part of her effort to keep colors light so that the space feels more open. The countertops are made of honed black granite, a matte finish that softens and lightens the effect of the dark horizontal surfaces, which would have seemed too harsh if they were highly polished. Both the floors and backsplash are finished in the same multicolored slate tile, since using the same material on both surfaces tends to expand the space visually, another kitchen design trick. Finally, the appliances are all stainless steel to give the eye some relief from the continuous line of wooden cabinets and to help open up the space.

Because of the clever space-conserving cabinet designs in the small area, contractor Alward was able to honor two of Stephanie's requests made at the onset of the project. At one end of the kitchen, he tucked in a tiny powder room, made even more efficient with the addition of a sliding door. On the wall that runs perpendicular to the kitchen's main galley, he created (from Gisslow's design) a built-in dining peninsula. By integrating the table into a storage credenza

Although the floor area of the old kitchen was slightly larger, it was hard to use and poorly organized. By creating lots of storage in odd places and straightening up the layout, the new kitchen packs more into less space.

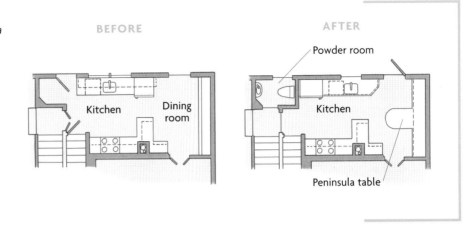

BEFORE

AFTER

Powder room

Kitchen

Dining room

Kitchen

Peninsula table

left Diagonal corner cabinets, such as the one next to the patio door, eliminate sharp corners and squeeze efficient storage out of limited space.

cutting-edge clean

■ Double-drawer dishwashers are one of the hottest appliance items available today. For households with one or two people, a two-drawer dishwasher can be an ideal way of avoiding the

twin banes of dishwashers: wasting energy by running them half full or waiting until they fill up and not having enough clean utensils. This one lets Stephanie run small loads, using one drawer at a time. She can also store dirty dishes in one drawer while she uses clean dishes from the other; then when the dirty drawer is full, she can turn on the dishwasher and reverse the roles.

along the back wall, Gisslow gave the table not only added function (as a place to work) but also freed up space that would have been hogged by a freestanding table and chairs.

The new kitchen perfectly suits both the house and its owner, creating a cozy, warm, and highly functional place for her to cook and eat, while honoring the attention to detail that went into the craftsmanship of the original house.

by building the dining table into a counter, the designer not only saved space but also created a handsome element that does double duty as a work surface.

1 This is one of six handy drawers designed under the counter.

2 A 3-in.-deep cabinet to the left of the range ensures that the space around a chimney chase is not wasted.

3 By choosing a separate oven and cooktop instead of an integrated range that contained both, the homeowner was able to mix and match features while keeping down space requirements.

1 Drawer

2 Shallow
storage door

3 Oven and
cooktop

resources

Architects and Designers

Joseph F. Augustine (p. 16)
JFA Architecture, P.C.
1017 Greenwood Ave.
Wyncote, PA 19095
215-517-8068
jaugustine@jfa-architecture.com

Bruce Bernbaum and Patricia Magadini (p. 110)
Bernbaum-Magadini Architects
4528 McKinney Ave., #103
Dallas, TX 75205
214-219-4528
www.bmarchitects.com

Erica Broberg (pp. 50, 60)
Erica Broberg Architect
25 Cedar St.
East Hampton, NY 11937
631-329-9928
www.ericabroberg.com

David Cadwallader (p. 110)
Cadwallader Design
1501 Dragon St.
Dallas, TX 75207
214-880-1777
dcadnt@att.net

Charles Cook (p. 84)
Myefski Cook Architects
716 Vernon Ave.
Glencoe, IL 60022
847-835-7081
www.myefskicook.com

Peter Duxbury, AIA (pp. 76, 152)
Duxbury Architects
382A First St.
Los Altos, CA 94022
650-917-3840
www.duxburyarchitects.com

Stephen Dynia (p. 142)
Stephen Dynia Architects
P.O. Box 4356, 4356 Maple Way
Jackson, WY 83001
307-733-3766
www.dynia.com

Irene Facciolo (pp. 68, 118)
Thunder Mill Design, Inc.
5 Winter St.
Montpelier, VT 05602
802-223-3112
www.thundermilldesign.com

Dennis Fox, AIA (p. 160)
Fox Design Group Architects
1116 Washington St., Ste. D
Richmond, CA 94801
510-235-3369
fdg@foxdesigngroup.com

Jennifer Gisslow, CKD (p. 174)
Design Source
1181 Begier Ave.
San Leandro, CA 94577
510-635-3963
jennie@designsrc.com

Virginia W. Kelsey, AIA (p. 24)
4545 Post Oak Pl., Ste. 365
Houston, TX 77027
713-524-8400
www.virginiakelsey.com

Jim Miller, AIA (p. 42)
Oculus Architecture and Design
1501 Powell St., Studio L
Emeryville, CA 94608
510-594-1814
oculus_architecture@yahoo.com

Hiro Morimoto (p. 166)
Morimoto Architects
1200 Tenth St.
Berkeley, CA 94710
510-527-8800
www.morimotoarch.com

Michael Mullin (pp. 92, 134)
Michael Mullin, Architect, Ltd.
95 Brady St.
San Francisco, CA 94103
415-626-1190
www.michaelmullin.com

Barry Peterson (p. 34)
Deliberate Design + Architecture
480 Gate 5 Rd., ICB Studio 200
Sausalito, CA 94965
415-332-1300
www.deliberate-design.net

Neil Sandvold, AIA (p. 128)
Sandvold Blanda Architecture +
Interiors
117 S. 17th St.
Philadelphia, PA 19103
215-636-0099
www.sandvoldblanda.com

Henry Siegel, FAIA (p. 102)
Siegel & Strain Architects
1259 59th St.
Emeryville, CA 94608
510-547-8092

Contractors

Tom Alderson (p. 166)
Alderson Construction
710 Channing Way
Berkeley, CA 94710
510-841-7159

Keith Alward (p. 174)
Alward Construction
780 San Luis Rd.
Berkeley, CA 94707
510-527-6498
www.alwardconstruction.com

Richard E. Bartels (p. 16)
Bartels Contracting
3423 Larch Rd.
Huntingdon Valley, PA 19006
215-947-7518

Bill English (p. 160)
English Construction
453 California St.
Point Richmond, CA 94801
510-232-7559

T.W. Heyenga Construction, Inc. (p. 76)
144 S. 3rd St., Unit 131
San Jose, CA 95112
408-275-8003

Phil Kline (p. 34)
315 Durant Way
Mill Valley, CA 94941
415-381-8097

Steve Kubik (p. 24)
8602 Westview Dr.
Houston, TX 77055
713-973-0302
skubik@houston.rr.com

Scott McCaslin (p. 110)
McCaslin Associates, Inc.
5011 McKinney Ave.
Dallas, TX 75205
214-520-2500

Gene Peterson (p. 92)
San Anselmo, CA 94960
415-823-4413

George Ryan (p. 118)
Ryan Construction
Brook Rd.
Barre, VT 05641
802-479-5584

Steve Schliff (pp. 42, 102)
On the Beam Remodeling
1585 32nd St.
Oakland, CA 94608
510-832-0144

Via Builders, Inc. (p. 152)
4600 El Camino Real
Los Altos, CA 94022
650-948-1077 x13

Appliances

Abbreviations:
ckt—cooktop
dw—dishwasher
mic—microwave
rd—refrigerator drawer
ref—refrigerator
rng—range
tc—trash compactor
vh—vent hood
wc—wine cooler
wd—warming drawer
wo—wall oven

Abbaka Vent Hoods (p. 134)
800-548-3932
www.abbaka.com

Amana® (p. 102, ref; p. 118, ref; p. 160, ref, rng; p. 174, ref)
800-843-0304
www.amana.com

**Bosch® (p. 16, ct, dw;
p. 34, dw; p. 134, dw;
p. 24, wo, dw, tc)**
800-921-9622
www.boschappliances.com

Broan® Vent Hoods (p. 24, vh)
800-558-1711
www.broan.com

**Dacor® (p. 110, wo, wd;
p. 76, ct, vh)**
800-793-0093
www.dacor.com

DCS™ (p. 50, rng, vh)
800-433-8466
www.dcsappliances.com

Dynasty by Jade® (p. 34, rng)
888-462-9824
www.jadeappliances.com

**Earthstone Wood-Fire Ovens
(p. 142, wo)**
800-840-4915
www.earthstoneovens.com

Faber® Vent Hoods (p. 60, vh)
508-358-5353
www.faberonline.com

**Fisher & Paykel Appliances Inc.
(p. 76, dw; p. 174, dw)**
888-936-7872
usa.fisherpaykel.com

Frigidaire® (p. 68, ref, dw)
800-374-4432
www.frigidaire.com

**General Electric® (p. 16, ref, mic;
p. 76, ref; p. 34, ref; p.60, rng, ref,
mic, wd, wc; p. 118, wo; p. 134,
ref; p. 128, mic; p. 84, ref)**
800-626-2000
www.geappliances.com

Jenn-Air® (p. 76, wo)
800-688-1100
www.jennair.com

**KitchenAid® (p. 110, mic, dw;
p. 84, wo; p. 166, wo, tc; p. 160,
dw)**
800-422-1230
www.kitchenaid.com

Maytag® (p.118, dw)
800-688-9900
www.maytag.com

**Miele® (p. 152, dw,wo; p. 128,
dw; p. 60, dw; p. 92, dw)**
800-843-7231
www.miele.com

**Sub-Zero® (p. 76, ref; p. 42, ref;
p. 152, ref; p. 128, ref, rd; p. 110,
ref; p. 166, ref; p. 24, ref)**
800-222-7820
www.subzero.com

**Thermador® (p. 16, wo; p. 68,
wo, ct, vh; p. 174, ct, wo, mic;
p. 142, rng,dw)**
800-656-9226
www.thermador.com

Wolf® (p. 166, ct; p. 84, ct)
800-332-9513
www.subzero.com/wolf

**Viking® (p. 92, ref, ct, rng, wc,
wo; p. 134, rng; p. 42, rng; p. 152,
rng; p. 128, rng; p. 60, rng;
p. 24, ct; p. 118, ct)**
888-845-4641
www.vikingrange.com

Cabinets

**Brookhaven® by Wood-Mode®
(p. 16)**
877-635-7500
www.wood-mode.com

Bulthaup® (p. 128)
212-966-7183
www.bulthaup.com

George DiGiulio (p. 34)
19356 Orange Ave.
Sonoma, CA 95476
707-996-9056

Dutchman Doors (p. 24)
Fremont, CA 94538
510-656-6166
www.dutchmandoors.com

**Huggy Bear's Cupboards®
(p. 174)**
503-289-5541
www.huggybear.com

Smith River Kitchens (p. 50)
25 Cedar St.
East Hampton, NY 11937
631-329-7122

Trumblewood (p. 160)
2707 8th St.
Berkeley, CA 94710
510-849-3599
trumblewood@aol.com

Wickets Fine Cabinetry (p. 84)
708 Vernon Ave.
Glencoe, IL 60022
847-835-0868
www.wicketscabinetry.com

Woodharbor® (p. 60)
641-423-0444
ww2.woodharbor.com

Countertops

CaesarStone (p. 102)
877-9QUARTZ
www.caesarstoneus.com

Corian (pp. 16, 76, 166)
800-426-7426
www.corian.com

IMC® Stone Company (p. 110)
www.stonemanufacturer.com

**John Boos™ Butcher Block
(p. 102)**
217-347-7701
www.johnboos.com

**Just Manufacturing Stainless
Steel (p. 34)**
www.justmfg.com

**Vermont Soapstone Company
(pp. 68, 92)**
802-263-5404
www.vermontsoapstone.com

Faucets and Sinks

Abbreviations:
f—faucet
s—sink

**American Standard®
(p. 160, s, f)**
800-442-1902
www.americanstandard-us.com

Blanco® (p. 102, s)
www.blancoamerica.com

**Chicago Faucets® (p. 68, f; p. 76,
f; p. 24, f)**
847-803-5000
www.chicagofaucets.com

Concinnity® Faucets (p. 118, f)
800-356-9993
www.concinnityusa.com

**Elkay® (p. 16, s, f; p. 76, s; p. 50,
s; p. 166, f, s; p. 174, s)**
630-574-8484
www.elkayusa.com

**Franke® Sinks & Faucets (p. 92,
s; p. 68, f; p. 42, f; p. 134, f, s; p.
152, s; p. 110, s; p. 24, s)**
800-626-5771
www.frankeksd.com

**Grohe® Faucets (p. 152, f; p. 84,
f; p. 102, f; p. 174, f)**
630-582-7711
www.groheamerica.com

**Kohler® Plumbing (p. 92, s;
p. 42, s; p. 60, s; p. 128, f)**
800-456-4537
www.us.kohler.com

KWC® Faucets (p. 110, f; p. 50, f)
678-334-2121
www.kwcfaucets.com

resources (continued)

Moen® (p. 84, s; p. 142, f)
800-289-6636
www.moen.com

Sigma® Faucets (p. 60)
760-598-5895
www.sigmafaucets.com

Tiles

Country Floors® (p. 24)
800-311-9995
www.countryfloors.com

Heath® Ceramic Tile (p. 76)
415-332-3732
www.heathceramics.com

Walker & Zanger® (p. 102)
713-300-2940
www.walkerzanger.com

Lighting

Alkco® Lighting (pp. 102, 160)
866-502-5526
www.alkco.com

Flos® (pp. 110, 128)
631-549-2745
www.flos.net

Halo® Lighting (p. 102)
770-486-4800
www.cooperlighting.com

Juno® (pp. 84, 160)
847-827-9880
www.junolighting.com

Lightolier® (pp. 16, 128)
508-679-8131
www.lightolier.com

Flooring Manufacturers

Forbo Marmoleum (p. 134)
800-842-7839
www.forbolinoleumna.com

Thorn Tree Slate (p. 24)
713-690-8200
www.thorntreeslate.com

Wicanders® Cork Flooring (p. 102)
410-553-6062
www.wicanders.com